JOHN WILKES BOOTH: A SISTER'S MEMOIR

John Wilkes Booth

JOHN WILKES BOOTH

A
SISTER'S
MEMOIR
by ASIA
BOOTH
CLARKE

EDITED AND WITH AN INTRODUCTION BY
TERRY ALFORD

University Press of Mississippi *Jackson*

The paper in this book meets the guidelines for permanence and dura-
bility of the Committee on Production Guidelines for Book Longevity
of the Council on Library Resources.

Library of Congress Cataloging-in-Publication Data

Clarke, Asia Booth, 1835-1888
    John Wilkes Booth : a sister's memoir / by Asia Booth Clarke ;
edited and with an introduction by Terry Alford.
        p.   cm.
    Rev. ed. of: The unlocked book. 1971.
    Includes bibliographical references and index.
    ISBN 0-87805-883-4 (cloth : alk. paper)
    1. Booth, John Wilkes, 1838–1865.   2. Booth family.   3. Lincoln,
Abraham, 1809–1865—Assassination.   I. Alford, Terry.   II. Clarke,
Asia Booth, 1835–1888. Unlocked book.   III. Title.
E457.5.C615   1996
973.7'092—dc20
[B]   96-18595
                                                                CIP

British Library Cataloging-in-Publication data available

Designed by Amanda K. Lucas

To the memory of
John C. Brennan (1908–1996),
friend and historian

CONTENTS

PREFACE

The assassination of President Abraham Lincoln on April 14, 1865, made the name of his assailant, John Wilkes Booth, familiar to the entire nation. Unlike the names of future presidential assassins, however, his was already known to much of the American public. Junius Brutus Booth, Sr., the assassin's father, had acted throughout the country since 1821. He enjoyed a long and distinguished career. The elder Booth's older sons, Junius, Jr., and Edwin, also actors, kept the name in lights after the father's death in 1852. Then, in early 1862, John Wilkes Booth established his own reputation as a nationally ranked performer. He toured widely, acting in all the principal cities of the nation. When a play called for a mysterious stranger, a fiendish tyrant, or a passionate swashbuckler, the handsome and athletic young Booth filled the bill—literally. Dramatic critics were mixed in their opinions of him. Some were lukewarm toward him while others were unstinting in their praise. The play-going public was less hesitant, embracing him without reserve. Soon Booth was earning twenty thousand dollars a year. By the time he quit his full-time stage career in May 1864, at the age of twenty-six, he had become one of the most popular and successful actors in the United States.

One need not search far in the historical record to find friendly recollections of John Wilkes Booth by his contemporaries. The actors and staff at Ford's Theatre thought the world of him. Gay and light-hearted, "he was nothing like his terrible deed suggests," claimed Kitty Brink, a wardrobe assistant and dresser. Actor John Matthews found Booth was "a most winning, captivating man." To W. J. Ferguson of Ford's he was "a marvelously clever and amusing demigod." Even members of the Ford family remembered him fondly, despite the hardships his murder of Lincoln brought them personally. John T. Ford felt he was a brilliant personality and actor with "Apollo's own grace about him." Younger brother Harry Ford, a particular friend, always insisted that Booth was "one of the simplest, sweetest-dispositioned, and most lovable men he ever knew."

There was astonishment among Booth's acquaintances when he shot Lincoln. John Ellsler, a theater manager and business partner of Booth's, was having breakfast in Columbus, Ohio, when the fearful news came from Washington. He sat frozen, unable to "move or speak." When "reaction finally came [to me], I was on fire. I could not, would not believe it." Comedian William Warren was on a train traveling from Manchester, New Hampshire, to Boston when he learned of the tragedy from a conductor rushing down the aisle. Unable to believe what he was hearing, Warren leaped to his feet and contradicted the man. It seemed impossible that Booth was an assassin. "Alas," Warren wrote in his diary, "it proved too true."

Ellsler and Warren may be forgiven their surprise. Many others who knew Booth were equally astonished. "It is a strange thing if he be guilty of this crime," one New York City editor wrote. "He is a young fellow of spirit, of acute mind, and of great professional vigor. . . . His temperament is romantic and poetical. His disposition has been considered as gentle. There are no circumstances or antecedents to mark him as a man likely to conceive or execute such a crime. His complicity in such a conspiracy appears to astound all who know him." A Chicago friend of Booth's agreed, adding he was not aware that Booth "could kill Lincoln or any other man." All knew Booth had the audacity to commit murder, but, as the editor of a theatrical newspaper expressed it, they "never thought he had the murderous heart, the moral poltroonery, and the inexpressible wickedness which stamps the assassin as the vilest of God's creatures."

Newspapers of 1865 were quick to offer their explanations. It was reported that Booth was acting for the Confederate government. He was their agent, their tool, or their fool. Perhaps he did it for money. Some writers sought personal motives, seeing an angry and vengeful nature in the young actor. Booth was said to be shallow, vain, and pathetic. He wanted fame but was too lazy to work for it. Perhaps his abuse of alcohol (and even drugs, it was rumored) fueled the murder. Or explained it. Family skeletons appeared. The public was told that Booth had inherited his father's well-documented mental instability. He was mad, then, not merely bad. Another writer informed the public that the assassin's parents were not legally married when the son was born, making Booth a bastard. He was, therefore, corrupt from the start. And what about Booth's connection to the theater? Wasn't the theater a world of false reality where cheaply obtained applause had flattered and corrupted Booth's dissolute personality?

Of all the writing on Booth from the turbulent days of 1865 to the present no document can offer the extraordinary insight into the assassin which the following memoir provides. The author was Booth's sister Asia, a poet and biographer. Her recollection, written in 1874, is the only lengthy account of Booth left by a family member. Since its publication in 1938, it has been recognized as indispensable to understanding the ill-fated young man. Certainly no outsider had Asia's insights into Booth's personality or could share such intimate personal knowledge about the gifted actor-assassin. Asia was a loyal sister who writes with affection and even indulgence. Her memoir is not and doubtlessly could not be an objective history. Its strengths compensate fully for this defect, however. And even Asia, in the end, cannot hide her horror at the consequences of the assassination for her brother and those who loved him.

ACKNOWLEDGMENTS

It is a pleasure to acknowledge my debt of gratitude to James O. Hall for his counsel and encouragement in my study of the life of John Wilkes Booth. Asia Booth Clarke's proposed epitaph for her brother John Wilkes—"Ever Faithful"—might be applied to Mr. Hall's steady course of seeking and sharing the truth about events of April 14, 1865.

To my colleagues David Herbert Donald, Stephen M. Archer, and Daniel C. Watermeier I am grateful for assistance in helping me resolve certain questions about the text. Their assistance, as well as their continued interest in my research on Booth, is appreciated. Ray Wemmlinger of the Hampden-Booth Theatre Library and Mary Markee of the Peale Museum were generous in their support of this project. Jonathan Mann and Richard and Kellie Gutman graciously provided photographs from their personal collections for use in the book.

Laura Noell, Bob Lesman, and Dick Pellerin, three friends and fellow laborers at Northern Virginia Community College, read and offered suggestions on an early draft of the editor's introduction. Friends indeed! They improved the final product significantly. And Linda Delp-Miller deserves sincere thanks for speeding the project along by sharing her time and her knowledge of computers.

The support of JoAnne Prichard of the University Press of Mississippi made this book possible. She was enthusiastic about it from the start and never wavered when progress was uncertain.

Lastly I would like to thank Putnam Publishing Group for permission to reprint certain portions of its title *The Unlocked Book: A Memoir of John Wilkes Booth by His Sister Asia Booth Clarke* (1938), published by G. P. Putnam's Sons, copyright 1938.

CHRONOLOGY OF THE LIFE OF
JOHN WILKES BOOTH

1838, May 10	Born at family farm near Bel Air, Harford County, Maryland
1840s	Attends various schools in Baltimore, Bel Air
1851–1852	Construction of Tudor Hall on farm near Bel Air
1852–1853	Attends St. Timothy's Hall Academy, Catonsville, Maryland
1852, November 10	Death of Junius Brutus Booth, Sr.
Mid-1850s	Lives at Tudor Hall; attempts farming
1855, August 14	Appears for first time on professional stage in Baltimore
1857, July	Tudor Hall and farm advertised for rent
1857–1858	Commences full-time career as apprentice actor at Arch Street Theatre, Philadelphia
1858–1860	Resident actor with Marshall Theatre stock company, Richmond
1859, November–December	Serves with First Virginia Regiment at Charles Town, [West] Virginia; witnesses execution of John Brown, December 2

1860, October–November	First tour with starring roles in Georgia, Alabama
1860, December	Rejoins family then living in Philadelphia
1861, January–April	Stars in several small northern cities
1861, April–May	Civil War commences; riots in Baltimore; northern pacification of Maryland commences
1862–1863	Stars in Chicago, New York, Baltimore, St. Louis, Boston and other cities; career at artistic and financial height
1863, November 9	President Lincoln attends Booth performance at Ford's Theatre, Washington
1864, May 27	Concludes last star engagement, Boston
1864, summer	Superintends oil investments at Franklin, Pennsylvania
1864, August	Initiates plot to abduct Lincoln as hostage for the South
1864, October	Visits Canada to ship theatrical wardrobe to South; meets Confederate agents
1864, November	Performs *Julius Caesar* with brothers at Winter Garden Theatre, New York; leaves "To Whom It May Concern" letter and letter to his mother at Asia's home

1865, March 17	Fails in attempt to abduct Lincoln in Washington
1865, April 14	Assassinates Lincoln at Ford's Theatre, escapes; Lincoln dies, April 15
1865, April 26	Killed at Garrett farm, Caroline County, Virginia
1865, April 27	Body identified formally, autopsied, and secretly buried in Washington
1869, February 15–17	Remains exhumed, taken to Baltimore for identification by family, and placed in receiving vault to await burial
1869, June 26	Reburial in family lot in Green Mount Cemetery, Baltimore

JOHN WILKES BOOTH: A SISTER'S MEMOIR

ASIA BOOTH CLARKE AND HER MEMOIR

The Editor's Introduction

Asia Booth, the author of this memoir, was born on the family farm near Bel Air, Maryland, on November 20, 1835. Her father was Junius Brutus Booth, Sr., thirty-nine years old and one of the nation's leading actors. Asia's mother was Mary Ann Holmes. The parents were English, having immigrated to the United States in 1821. It was many months before the couple chose a name for the child, being undecided "whether to call her after the accomplished young [actress] Sydney Cowell (Mrs. Bateman), who was a great favorite with Mr. and Mrs. Booth, or Ayesha, in recollection of one of Mahomet's wives." At length Junius wrote to his wife, "Call the little one *Asia* in remembrance of that country where God first walked with man, and *Frigga*, because she came to us on Friday . . . ," the day consecrated to the Norse goddess who presided over marriage and the home.[1]

The log farmhouse in which Asia was born was a crowded place in the 1830s. In addition to the parents the unpretentious structure was home to Asia's eccentric grandfather Richard Booth, a retired London lawyer. Older siblings Junius, Jr., Rosalie, and Edwin T. Booth, also shared the home.[2] Of these children "Ned" (as Edwin was often called) was close enough to Asia's age to be a playfellow, and the sister grew to idolize him. Younger brothers John Wilkes and Joseph Adrian soon came along, completing the number of six Booth children who would live to adulthood. Early in 1838 Asia's aunt Jane Booth Mitchell, her husband, and their seven children arrived from England to live for a time at the farm. If one includes Joe and Ann Hall, the African-American couple who lived with the Booth family, the Hall children, and the indeterminable number of black and white servants and hands who came and went over the years, the Booth place must have bulged at its seams from time to time.

The Booth family had also rented a house in Baltimore for some years. The father finally purchased one there in 1845.[3] It was an attractive three-story structure located in a quiet residential neighborhood on North Exeter Street. Although Junius Brutus Booth, Sr., loved the rural life, he found a home in the city more convenient for the frequent travelling his profession demanded. The city also offered superior educational opportunities for the children. Accordingly, the family would split its time between Baltimore and the farm near Bel Air, some twenty-five miles north of the city.

Only a few facts are known about Asia's education. Along with her brothers Edwin, John Wilkes, and Joseph, she spent some time at the "old-fashioned" school of Susan Hyde. Stressing the basics, Hyde presided over the school as if it were, in Asia's phrase, "her little circle." In a letter written more than forty years later, Edwin characterized the ever-patient Hyde as a "dear old school-marm" and "a woman all through—in the true sense of that word—gentle in manner, soft in heart, and low in her estimation of her worth."[4]

It was at the Hyde school that Asia met her future husband, John Clarke Sleeper. "Jack" Sleeper was a neighborhood boy whose mother ran a hotel. He grew very attached to Edwin and became his "good angel," according to John T. Ford, owner (in the 1860s) of Ford's Theatre in Washington, D.C. One day when Hyde kept Edwin after school, Ford recalled, Jack waited anxiously for him, pacing back and forth across the street. Hyde looked out and saw he was holding a brick. She called to him and asked what he was doing. "I thought you were going to whip Edwin," he replied to her astonishment, "and the moment you laid a hand on him, I was going to throw this brick through the window at you."[5]

Soon the loyal Jack was walking Asia to school, her books in his arms.

Martin J. Kerney was Asia's next teacher. His school was held in a small brick building located just along Exeter Street from the Booth home. Kerney lacked humility of the Hyde variety but he was no less excellent as a teacher. Energetic, ambitious, and civic-minded, Kerney stressed the language arts and encouraged his students in public speaking. It was at his school that Edwin and Jack Sleeper, both wearing white trousers and black jackets, enacted the quarrel scene between Brutus and Cassius from Shakespeare's *Julius Caesar*.[6] Oddly attired as these "Romans" were, they wowed a schoolroom crowded with a "not overly-critical audience of mammas, papas, and other relatives." The elder Booth, who opposed a stage career for his children, slipped in unobserved and watched from a back bench. He seemed pleased.

Asia left a paragraph of notes on an unnamed "college for young girls" where she also studied at an unspecified period.[7] In this unusual place, an all-girls' school taught by men only, there were no class distinctions. All the students were thrown together and all were taught alike. Moreover, "the scholars were made to imitate the manners and pursue the studies of boys." Students were addressed by their last names only, with no polite prefix. They read, wrote, and debated continually. Standing on a staircase, a girl would recite while her classmates sat below listening, and a teacher, his back braced against a door, stood with book in hand to follow along and voice corrections. Geology and botany were taught on long walks about Baltimore. Ball games, races, jumping, archery, and even kite flying during the windy months were part of the program.

Perhaps in reaction to the freewheeling spirit of this "college," Asia was next enrolled in a school run by the Sisters of the Carmelite Convent on Aisquith Street. Kerney, an important Catholic layman and author, may have encouraged her attendance. Although she received much of her formal education at this place and its influence was profound, Asia left almost no record of the time she passed here beyond noting that the cloistered nuns had "a small wooden skull in their cells to keep Death, if not in their dreams, at least in their bed-rooms."[8]

Asia in her mid-teens was a slender young woman with a proud nature and a literary turn of mind. She loved to write poetry and was adept at turning family events into verse. She was equally talented as a correspondent. Her letters to Junius Jr.'s daughter Blanche were said by a third party who read them to "evince a high order of intellect, combined with an amiable disposition and heart."[9] Asia was "a very smart woman, by the by," stated one New York City columnist, "educated and mathematical, somewhat of a writer, and tremendously 'strong-minded.'"[10] She had her share of female friends and no shortage of male admirers either. "I think I never heard anyone who knew her mention her name without adding, 'She was a beautiful woman,'" wrote Ella Mahoney, an early historian of the family.[11] Sociable and intelligent, Asia was as talkative as older sister Rosalie was quiet, or so the joke in the family went. Unhappily, she could also be touchy and inflexible. A small incident might send her sulking. "These hours of self-inflicted torment were filled with anger against everyone," Asia wrote of herself. Her father cautioned everyone to leave her alone on these occasions since "no reasoning would melt a sulky temper."[12]

Asia's personality is further revealed in a series of letters written over the years to her close friend Jean Anderson. The letters show a romantic, passionate, and restless nature, remarkably like that of her brother John. Asia might also be volatile. Of an acquaintance who was spreading unpleasant rumors, Asia declared to Jean, "I'd like to write a letter on her face with this pen." And when Edwin escorted a young woman of whom Asia disapproved to Niagara Falls, she expressed the hope that the young woman would "go under the Falls or try to swim in the whirlpool." Generally, however, her letters are filled with pleasant news, chit-chat, and the doings of friends and family ("Joe goes to school in Elkton . . . John is trying to farm"). Depressed when a love relationship floundered, she confided to Jean, "I trust I shall never become what I detest, a scrupulous, prudish, cold-hearted narrow judging woman. I want to be a kind, good, generous, a merciful philanthropic old maid." She daydreamed of going to a convent. "Some loving hand" was beckoning her there, she thought. "Oh Jean, my Jean, all is vanity," she wrote shortly before her twenty-first birthday. "How little is there real and earnest, pure and genuine in life." One letter was signed "the same sad Asia." The last words she records as having been spoken to her by her brother John seem appropriate: "Try to be happy."[13]

On November 30, 1852, Junius Brutus Booth, Sr., died on a Mississippi River steamboat near Louisville, Kentucky, as he was returning home from an acting tour to California.[14] His wife, Mary Ann, travelled alone to Cincinnati to claim his body. It lay in state in Baltimore in the parlor of the North Exeter Street home, the corpse so lifelike in appearance that it drew forth hopeful exclamations that Booth was only in a trance. A physician was summoned to confirm the obvious. Asia would write that "people of every class" soon filled the home to express their sympathy. Many followed the family in a funeral procession through the snowy streets to the Baltimore Cemetery.

The father had been a trusting man of "unquestioning philanthropy [and] an almost childlike faith in the honesty of human nature," his daughter recalled. Accordingly there was little money left at his death. Since city life was expensive and the family no longer had an income, Mary Ann decided to rent the North Exeter residence. "What a bright, happy home it was," Asia wrote to Jean, "broken up forever." Back to the farm went the Booths. A new house of neo-Gothic design, conceived by the father as a retirement home, had been constructed there.[15] Asia named this grand cottage Tudor Hall. With Junius, Jr., and Edwin living in California and Joseph often away at boarding school, the new house now became home to Mary Ann, Rosalie, Asia and John Wilkes. Loyal to his father's wishes, the remaining son began to farm.

These years of the mid-1850s form the heart of the following memoir. In the relative isolation of the Maryland countryside Asia and John became constant companions. When the demanding common labor of house and farm was done, the two would pass their time in horseback riding, village dances, picnics, camp meetings and walks in the "wild old woods" nearby. Close in age, they shared their love of poetry and music. Long talks on the porch or before the fire filled the evening hours. Here they were "lonely together," as Asia expressed it.[16] About them everywhere were reminders of a father whose memory evoked a further sharing, of pride in his acting fame and shame over his eccentricities. A strong bond of sympathy between brother and sister developed in these years. The following pages are forever a testament to their mutual devotion.

Jack Sleeper would visit the farm occasionally. He had pursued Asia patiently through the years. An oft-told story of their courtship—that she would not promise to marry him unless he chose acting for his profession—seems unlikely. Asia's beau had wanted a theatrical career ever since he had known the Booths. In the summer of 1850 he and Edwin had given a performance at the courthouse in Bel Air to what Sleeper described as "an eager throng of bumpkins." When the elder Booth expressed himself pleased with his acting and added, "I could not believe it was in you," Sleeper felt the remark firing "my boyish ambition to adopt the profession of the stage."[17] He went on to study law for a time at his mother's insistence but abandoned it soon enough and took his first regular engagement at the Chestnut Street Theatre in Philadelphia in August 1852. An actor not wishing to be thought of as a *Sleeper* in any way, he reversed his middle and last names, being reborn to the world as John Sleeper Clarke.

Gossip columnist Harry Hill wrote that Asia believed "every woman is the born superior of every man, and that it is a piece of condescension for any female to play wife to a mere man's [role as] husband."[18] While Asia could be difficult, the statement is unfriendly and untrue. As the years went on, marriage between Asia and John Sleeper Clarke seemed to assume an inevitability. Edwin's fiancee, Mary Devlin, worried that Asia was too superior intellectually to her husband.[19] But Edwin was fiercely in favor of the match, and Asia wrote later (and not clearly in jest), "I married to please him." No one in the Booth family opposed the marriage—with one exception. John took leave from an acting engagement he had undertaken in Richmond to attend his sister's wedding. "Not pleased at my marriage," the younger brother whispered words of caution to Asia that she later found prophetic. Or so she said. Nevertheless he was prominently in place on the morning of April 28, 1859, when Asia and Clarke were married at historic St. Paul's Episcopal Church in Baltimore.[20]

In her new home in Philadelphia Asia was truly happy, at least for a time. "The best and kindest friend," Clarke was an attentive husband who left books and other small gifts for his bride. Soon what Asia called her "little trotters" came along— seven children in a ten-year period. "John [Wilkes] Booth laughs outrageously at me for having babies," Asia wrote Jean. "He can't realize it, he says, to think that our Asia should be a mother. He lies on the floor and rolls over with them like a child." In early 1863 John won "a beautiful set of baby clothes at a fair out west and made me a present of them. Need I be more explicit and say the gift was very appropriate?" Asia asked Jean. Each pregnancy seemed to be followed immediately by another. "I am sorry to be in such a strait again," she lamented. "Don't be in a hurry to turn a lover into a husband."

As Asia struggled with the demands of motherhood, Clarke made progress in the theater.[21] Although he desired to play drama, it was apparent that his forte was comedy. This was a happy fact, for "life struck his mind at a comic angle," thought critic William Winter.[22] Blessed with health and energy, Clarke had an expressive face, a quick step, and a powerful voice that could be heard clearly throughout the theater. His knowledge of human nature was ready made for exploitation by his wit and sense of mimicry. Clarke specialized in *low comedy*, a type of comedy which was clownish, ridiculous, or farcical in nature. The silly plots and buffoonish characters of low comedy made for irresistibly diverting entertainment. Playgoers roared with laughter when Clarke popped out on stage as a bug-eyed drunk wearing a red fright wig, or when, dressed as a housewife, he placed food absentmindedly on chairs where other people were about to sit. The mere sight of Clarke coming on stage would often produce laughter. In the spring of 1861, the *New York Clipper*, the nation's leading theatrical newspaper, crowned him "the only low comedian of importance in the country."[23]

As Clarke made his climb in the profession, he also proved skillful in another area. "The business quality and habit of accumulating were developed in him to a far greater degree than is usual even among the prudent and successful members of his profession," wrote a contemporary.[24] Deciding to make money on both ends of the business, he got a start in management at the Arch Street Theatre in Philadelphia in 1858. In October 1863, he and Edwin purchased that city's Walnut Street Theatre. "Feeling that they would be lucky to be able to pay for it in thirteen years," Asia boasted, the partners were able to burn their mortgage only three years later.[25] The following summer they added to their ventures the management of New York's Winter Garden Theatre, all the while fully engaged in their own acting schedules. Far from suffering under the load, Clarke's career boomed. During the 1864–1865 season "his triumphs of comedy [brought out] the whole town," declared the *New York Dramatic News*.[26]

Life had been a dizzying succession of personal and professional fulfillments for the couple—until the fateful Saturday of April 15, 1865. Clarke was shaving that morning, preparing for the day. In bed in a nearby room Asia rested, midway through a demanding pregnancy with twins. Suddenly the husband heard a horrifying scream from his wife. Rushing to her, Clarke found

Asia in great distress as she pointed to the morning newspaper which had just been brought in. The headlines announced that John Wilkes Booth had murdered President Abraham Lincoln the preceding evening in Washington. A. K. McClure, a family friend, wrote later that no words his skill as a journalist might employ could possibly describe the shock of this blow to the couple. Clarke struggled "to calm [Asia's] hysterical agony," feeling his own anxiety mount rapidly at the same time.[27]

A telegram to Edwin's home in New York summoned Mrs. Booth. The mother arrived by train late that same afternoon, crushed in spirit and showing all of her sixty-two years. "Poor mother," Junius wrote to Edwin, "who can console her, for a mother is a mother ever, and I am afraid she can never be brought to look calmly on this dreadful calamity."[28] The day ended with the entire household in anguish and dread.

In the large home which Asia described as "an extensive old mansion," the Clarkes kept an iron safe. John had been accustomed for safety's sake to leave important papers there as he toured the country. One such packet lay in the safe. The family remembered it on Sunday. Pulling open the heavy wooden door and an inner metal second door, they retrieved a large sealed envelope. Inside the envelope were federal and city bonds worth four thousand dollars, an assignment to Junius, Jr., of Pennsylvania oil land which the assassin owned, and certain other papers.[29] Of exceptional personal interest were a letter to his mother, retracting his promise to her to stay clear of the war, and a lengthy political manifesto written to justify his earlier effort to abduct President Lincoln and carry him as a prisoner into the Confederacy. (Both documents are reproduced in a later section of the book.)

Clarke had no sympathy for the rebellion and even less for John. He would tell the distinguished English comedian Sir Charles Wyndham that once during the war Booth had attacked him physically when he disparaged the South.[30] Feeling that Booth's letter to his mother would exculpate his own household and himself from any connection with the murder, Clarke "instantly desired [that it] should be made public." On Tuesday evening, April 18, Clarke and his friend John D. Stockton, an editor of the *Philadelphia Press*, presented Booth's letters to William Millward, the United States marshal for the eastern district of Pennsylvania. Reading them, Millward realized that publication of Booth's labored but affectionate letter to his mother would be "entirely inexpedient and improper . . . lest it create undue and false sympathy for the writer."[31] He suppressed it, but he did permit the press to publish instead the rambling treatise on North-South affairs Booth had composed in 1864 at the time his kidnap plot against Lincoln was active.

As Asia had feared, this ill-advised publication brought fresh misery on the family. "It not only served for food to newsmongers and enemies," she wrote, "but it directed a free band of male and female detectives to our house."[32] On the morning after the letter was printed, the residence was searched for Booth, who was still a fugitive. Then it was surrounded by a large complement of police and searched again. Marshal Millward led the charge through the mansion, taking away an empty packet bearing Asia's name in her brother's hand and other items deemed suspicious. A guard settled around the house. When Junius, Jr., arrived from Cincinnati, having narrowly escaped a mob in that city on the morning after the assassination, Clarke was noticeably inhospitable. "A *Booth* entering my house might cause a talk," he remarked coldly to his distressed brother-in-law.[33] Indignant at the comment, Junius demanded that the authorities be notified of his arrival in the city. They were, and Millward reappeared. He found Junius in bed, exhausted and disheartened.

Several days later more lightning struck when Junius learned that serious misconstructions were being put on a letter he had written to his brother two days before the assassination. Officials found covert meanings in a comment he made about John's oil business. Junius was arrested on April 25 and brought to Washington. He was incarcerated "in close confinement" in the Carroll Annex of the Old Capitol Prison on April 26, the very day his fugitive brother was tracked down and shot to death in a Virginia barn by soldiers.[34] On the same day, Clarke was being arrested in Philadelphia, apparently as an afterthought. Three officers took him away. He was brought into the prison on April 27. The "Morning Report" of the Old Capitol Prison, carefully preserved at the National Archives, notes simply, "Clark, Jno. S., comedian, 32, Phila., Pa., [arrested] Apr. 26, by order of the president, per Pro[vost] Mar[shal James B.] Fry." Officially the two actors were designated as "Prisoners of State."[35]

It appears from Asia's account that she, too, was wanted in Washington, but upon producing a physician's certificate attesting to her inability to travel, she was spared the ordeal. A male detective was stationed briefly in her home. Although considerate, this officer was conscientious, following Asia from room to room, inspecting her mail, and trying to draw her into conversation. Time seemed to stand still for her under these oppressive conditions. Clarke was finally released on May 27 and Junius a few weeks later. No formal charges were ever made against either man. The two were simply dismissed. With their return to Philadelphia the family could begin to pick up the pieces.

Asia's twins, a boy and a girl, were born on August 20, 1865. She had promised her brother John that the next male child would be named for him. That being impossible now, the little boy was named Creston Clarke. He would grow up to become a talented and well-known actor. Although he could not bear John's name, he looked very much like his ill-fated uncle. The needs of Creston and his siblings were a salvation for Asia, pulling her into the present and away from preoccupation with grief. "It is dreadful to have no babies," she wrote to Jean.

Asia found added comfort as well in completing work on a biography of her father. This was a vindication of the elder Booth, whose alcoholism and bouts of mental illness were legendary among the nation's theatergoers. Asia, with John, had begun this task in 1853. The younger brother having neither the patience nor aptitude for such a project, the undertaking soon had became solely hers. Her mother discouraged the idea actively, burning letters useful to the work despite the daughter's shrill pleas. But Asia persevered. She collected what materials she could, talked to friends of her father, and leafed through old newspapers. She even visited James Mitchell, an uncle who had been cut off by the family after his neglectful treatment of his wife, her father's sister. This elderly oddball, living a solitary existence in a dingy Baltimore garret, provided her with valuable playbills and published criticisms of the father's acting career.[36]

The biography, when nearly complete, was forced aside by the demands of family life. Then came the assassination. Now it was more urgent than ever for Asia to vindicate the family's reviled name. "My task never should have been resumed," she wrote pointedly in her introduction, "but in the heaviest hours of our sorrow, so many tongues were free to calumniate us, privately and professionally, that I am urged to complete my work, in the belief that . . . this truthful sketch may tend to interest the friends of my lamented father. . . ."[37] In the book Asia mentioned Junius, Rosalie, Edwin, Joseph, and herself by name, but not John at any point. The dedication was to Mary Ann, whose "name, so hallowed and revered, is but a synonym of sorrow." The manuscript was published under the title *Booth Memorials. Passages, Incidents, and Anecdotes in the Life of Junius Brutus Booth, (the Elder.) By His Daughter.* Carleton Publishers of New York copyrighted the title on December 14, 1865. The book's title page carries the date of 1866. It was all the proud daughter could do for the present "to confute the aspersions of evil men" about her family.

Another great solace to Asia at this time was her conversion to Roman Catholicism. During her childhood no one church had been preeminent in the Booth household. Her father had been a free spirit, receptive to the best teachings of all religions. On Sundays he would walk with Asia through Baltimore, en-

joying the splendor of a flight of migrating birds or the quiet-
ness of a deserted wharf. The mother was more traditional,
having been raised in the Church of England and attending
the Episcopal Church in America. Evangelical neighbors told
Asia and her mother that they did not really consider the
Booths to be Christians. The family cared nothing for such
an opinion, leaving the children free to attend a variety of
churches. It is not suprising that Kerney and the Carmelites
had their influence. Asia scandalized one set of busybodies in
1852 by informing them that she went "to [Catholic] Mass in
the morning and to some Protestant church or meeting in the
afternoon." Her 1859 wedding, as already noted, took place in
an Episcopal church. Then came the frightful events of 1865.
They brought to a crisis Asia's need for a sense of legitimacy
and order. The date of her confirmation is not known. However,
much may be inferred from records of the Cathedral Basilica
of Saints Peter and Paul in Philadelphia.[38] These indicate
that Asia's children were baptized in a period of less than two
years starting shortly after Lincoln's assassination. A theatrical
newspaper noted in the later years of her life that she "was a
devout Roman Catholic, and very attentive to the duties of
her church."[39]

There was a final step which Asia could take to gain further
freedom from the aftereffects of the assassination. It was the
desperate step of emigration. Feeling that the United States
had seen its best days, she wrote to her friend Jean less than a
month after Lincoln's death that she did not care how soon she
turned her back upon the country. The idea appealed to Clarke
as well. Even before the assassination had made his family the
subject of malicious interest, Clarke had been anxious to win
a reputation on the lucrative London stage. He had even taken
Asia and their oldest daughter, Dolly, to England in April 1862,
but for some reason returned home without having performed.
At last, in October 1867, Clarke made his debut before an
appreciative London audience. He liked his prospects in the
city and decided to move there.

Asia spent the early months of 1868 packing and closing down her huge Philadelphia home. Her "little trotters" were now five in number: Dolly, also called Asia, aged eight; Edwin, seven; Adrienne, four; Creston, two; and Wilfred, whose first birthday would occur in the coming June. (Creston's twin sister, Lillian, had died in 1866.)[40] Asia wrote Jean that she wished to visit Baltimore "to bid you and the dear old nuns goodbye," but her responsibilities, uncertain health, and winter weather conspired against it. "I know you will be sorry to have me on the other side of the water, although we seldom see each other now," she wrote. Other farewells were more difficult, the parting with Mary Ann being "very bad" indeed. In New York Asia secured tickets to Liverpool for herself and four children only, little Edwin having gone ahead to England with his father. The mother, together with Dolly, Adrienne, Creston, Wilfred, and an unnamed servant, took passage on the Royal Mail Steamship *Russia.* Younger brother Joseph Booth was to have come along but did not since Asia "was independent enough to start out alone." On March 18, 1868, Asia and the children sailed for Europe.[41] She had written to Jean that she might be gone for two years, possibly three. Clearly she had no idea that the farewell glimpse she took over the ship's stern at the receding shoreline was the last look she would ever have of her native country.

"A pleasant smooth voyage" of nine days brought the little family to Liverpool. Clarke was there to greet them, and all seemed well. He had secured a furnished cottage outside of London for the family. "Surrounded by blooming flowers and fresh air," Asia felt revived there. "I feel so full of fresh spirits and nerve," she wrote. " . . . I think I shall like [England] very much, and hope to enjoy better health and get strong in this more congenial climate."

In the coming years Clarke did flourish. "No actor has come to us from the United States with a gift of humor which has so thoroughly caught the fancy of the English playgoing public," wrote the London critic E. L. Blanchard in 1870.[42]

Charles Dickens and others joined the praise. They loved his clever portrayals of human foibles from the silly inebriate to the pompous windbag. His role of "Dr. Pangloss" in *The Heir at Law* ran for a whopping one hundred and fifty nights in 1871. Soon here, as in America, he feathered his nest by adding management duties to stage ones. In 1878 he became lessee of the popular Haymarket Theatre. "John C. Clarke is a godsend to London," declared Clement Scott in an 1885 issue of *Theatre*.[43]

"Clarke was a dear, kind fellow," recalled actor Edward H. Sothern.[44] He had his peculiarities, like the odd habit of gliding into any nearby shop in order to avoid having to speak with people on the street. He avoided even friends like Sothern's father, Edward A. Sothern, at one time manager of the Haymarket. The elder Sothern was delighted to see Clarke do this for he in turn would hasten to the shop doorway and trap the comedian inside, lingering up to an hour until the exasperated Clarke was forced to come forth and be greeted "with great surprise." Despite his odd behavior, Clarke liked the Sotherns immensely. On Sundays he would call with his children at their home to take them for a drive. Clarke and Sothern took the lead vehicle. The Clarke children came behind them in two additional cabs. They were followed by Sothern's servant and dogs in a fourth cab, young Sothern and his siblings in a fifth hansom, and the father's sister trailing everyone in her own Victoria. This odd procession of six or even seven vehicles would roll down Oxford Street to Piccadilly, then out into the country for dinner by the river or for some adventure. These Haymarket years, Clarke reminisced in 1895, were "the happiest years of my life."[45]

Asia knew she was the object of envy to some, living abroad in a comfortable home, with servants, trips to the continent and material luxuries. Yet she found little that was enviable in her situation. By choice her life was confined to her home and family. She was "personally unknown in London, save to a very few trusted friends."[46] Lonely and increasingly ill with rheumatism, she grew to detest London. In an 1874 letter to

Jean she ripped into everything from the people to the climate to the food. "I hate fat, greasy-voiced, fair-whiskered Britons with all my heart," she wrote. She seemed especially offended that women were regarded as "inferior and second-rate creatures altogether." Yet it was impossible to think of returning to the United States. Clarke loved London and thrived there since he didn't require "pure air, sunshine or light of day," as she phrased it. Even a short visit to America would necessitate the hardships of an ocean voyage and the cruelty of reawakening the feelings of her mother who had grown reconciled to her absence. Asia knew, therefore, that she must stay. Each July 4 and February 22 (Washington's birthday) she would hang out "my Star Spangled banner" and keep the days as holidays in her household. "I have everything I desire [here] but home," she lamented.

Clarke made regular professional visits to the United States in the 1870s and 1880s, but always alone. He told his friend A. K. McClure of Philadelphia that "because of her infirm health and great suffering during sea voyages," his wife could not come with him. "It was hard for him to say that," McClure observed. "Between the lines could be well understood the fact that Mrs. Clarke could never entertain the idea of visiting the United States where the crime of her brother would be on every tongue."[47] Even in London it was impossible to escape the past. Creston Clarke grew up in ignorance of his uncle's act. Then, when he was ten years old, he was teased about the murder by some American boys. Dumbfounded, he ran home to his mother and asked her what the boys meant. With tears in her eyes, Asia could only respond, "Ask your father." Creston did "and then for the first time learned the story that had brought consuming and ineffaceable sorrow to his parents," wrote McClure.

Regrettably Clarke and Asia were growing less and less supportive of each other emotionally. According to Asia, Clarke had spoken to her of a divorce after the assassination in 1865. As additional children came along and the move to England took place, things may have settled down for a while. However, by the time Asia wrote the accompanying memoir of her brother (1874), she felt a clear sense of betrayal at her husband's lack of constancy. The estrangement deepened. Soon Asia wrote to Edwin that Clarke kept a private room at the theater and often slept there. If he came home, it was late when all were asleep. "He lives in mystery and silence as far as I am concerned. He lives a free going bachelor life and does what he likes." Some of Clarke's time was evidently being shared with another woman. Asia believed that as soon as she and the children left for a vacation in France, Clarke and his mistress would travel the English countryside together.[48]

Asia's anger at Clarke boiled over in a letter written to Edwin on June 3, 1879.[49] "I am so tired of his dukelike haughtiness—his icy indifference, and so disgusted with the many false things he tells me . . . ," she wrote. Edwin was then receiving sympathy after escaping an attempt on his life made by a crazed fan. Asia reported that her husband reacted with jealousy and a "long tirade on the wonderful Booths who get all the notoriety without *suffering!!* for it, he said. 'Look at me,' [Clarke continued], 'I was *dragged* to prison—and Edwin goes scot-free, gets all the fame . . . who thinks of what I endured.'" Asia believed that if Clarke had "never rushed into print with [John's 'To Whom It May Concern'] letter, he would never have gone to prison. . . . I never say it to him now—having said it once, and wrought him up to fury pitch. . . . It is marvelous how he hates me—the mother of nine babies—but I am a *Booth*—that is sufficient."

A "bachelor in all but name," Clarke had limited involvement with his "nine babies." Three additional children had been born after the move to England—daughter Joan and two others whose names are not known. All died. As was her way in the face of tragedy, Asia picked up her pen. She began a revision of the 1865 biography of her father, adding to it a companion life of her beloved brother Edwin. This was published in 1882 as part of the "American Actor Series" under the title *The Elder and the Younger Booth.* She also wrote and prepared printed proofs for a manuscript titled *Personal Recollections of the Elder Booth,* containing family stories, several charmingly told. Laurence Hutton, her editor for the "American Actor Series" volume, thought the nature of this work would "destroy the harmony" of the more formally written dual biography if issued with it.[50] It was, accordingly, not included in the new book, and in 1885 Asia gave the proof sheets to her son Wilfred. As for her poems, she had written to Edwin on several occasions about her dream "to publish them for the benefit of the Carmelites" of Baltimore.[51] The project seemed dependent upon her husband returning five hundred dollars of her money. The verses were never published.

Asia had written once to her friend Jean that she was getting "hardened to sorrow . . . like poor mother." But misfortune was not finished with her. Edwin Booth Clarke was the favorite child of both parents. Fluent in German before his eighth birthday, little Eddie was as precocious as he was handsome and gentle. His proud father attempted to secure him an appointment to the United States Naval Academy at Annapolis, Maryland, in 1878.[52] The young man was not admitted, however, and one story gave as the reason his being the nephew of Lincoln's assassin. Eddie became an officer in the British merchant navy instead. On December 10, 1881, while on a voyage from Australia, he was lost at sea.[53] His uncle and namesake Edwin Booth prayed that the news of his death was in error, more for his sister's sake than anyone else's. It was all too true, however. After everything else that had happened, Eddie's death was a devastating spirit-breaker for the mother.

Asia died on May 16, 1888, at Bournemouth, "a watering place on the southern coast of England" where she had gone to recuperate her health.[54] She was fifty-two years old. A valiant struggle with progressive heart disease, waged for several years, was over. Urgent cables to the United States had summoned her son Creston, who had embarked on his own acting career, and her husband Clarke. The two had hurried across the ocean, arriving in time to spend the last several days with her. Before she died, Asia had extracted a promise from Clarke to carry her body home to America and bury her with the Booths. All was done as she wished. On June 1, 1888, a small private service was held at the family plot in Green Mount Cemetery in Baltimore.[55] Along with her husband and son Creston, her surviving brothers Edwin and Joseph attended. They were all that remained of the immediate family. John T. Ford was among the mourners present. Asia's body had been placed in a white oak coffin adorned by roses in the shape of a small cross. The coffin was lowered into the earth, and the grave was slowly filled. Flowers were then piled on the mound of dirt that covered it.

Asia had come home at last. A few steps away from her final resting place was that of John Wilkes Booth. Death had reunited brother and sister. They had been so close in life. Now John and Asia were together again, this time as companions forever.

The memoir which follows was written in 1874, six years into Asia's English exile. The original consists of 132 pages of text inside a small black leather volume. Each page is filled with Asia's distinctive sloping handwriting. It appears that the memoir was composed over a relatively short period of time. Later Asia returned to the book occasionally to make a few insertions and additions, but the work was essentially complete. The manuscript had no title. The initials "J. W. B." were tooled on the book's cover in ornate gold lettering.[56]

Asia hoped that the memoir might be published, but that was out of the question in her lifetime. The wounds of the assassination were too fresh for an intimate portrayal of the man considered the most notorious murderer in American history. Furthermore, her husband would never have permitted such a book to appear. Asia discussed the manuscript with B. L. Farjeon, a popular English writer for whom she had a profound regard. Farjeon had theatrical connections through his marriage to Maggie Jefferson, daughter of the veteran American comedian Joseph Jefferson. The Farjeon family thought of Asia as "a sad and noble woman." Clarke was "mean." They had a deep respect for Lincoln, of course, but through their friendship with Asia they had developed some sympathetic understanding of his assassin as well. As a daughter of B. L. Farjeon wrote later, "Whatever feeling imbued for us the shadowy shape evoked by the name of John Wilkes Booth, it was never dissociated from compassion."[57]

Asia knew "that if the memoir of Wilkes fell into her husband's hands it would be destroyed." On her deathbed she directed the manuscript be given to Farjeon "to publish some time if he sees fit." A black tin box containing the document was duly presented to the noted author by Asia's daughter Dolly in June, 1888. Farjeon recognized the historical merits of the manuscript immediately but realized also the impropriety of publishing it during the lifetime of Asia's husband and brother. Edwin Booth died a few years later, in 1893, and Clarke in 1899. Farjeon then approached his father-in-law about the prospects of securing an American publisher for the memoir. The eminent Jefferson, a close friend of Edwin and an early patron of John, was not encouraging, and the project was dropped.

A generation later Farjeon's daughter Eleanor became interested in the manuscript. She felt enough time had passed from the events of 1865 to permit a proper reception for the work. The younger Farjeon prepared an edition which restored to the manuscript certain unflattering references to Clarke deleted in an earlier draft prepared by her father. To this she added an introduction and an appendix of clippings Asia had accumulated. In 1938, sixty years after Asia had died, her wish for the memoir finally came true when G. P. Putnam's Sons published the work under the title *The Unlocked Book: A Memoir of John Wilkes Booth by His Sister Asia Booth Clarke*.

Two additional generations have now passed since the original printing, and the need for an entirely new edition has become evident. People, events, and cultural references well known to Asia and her contemporaries have grown less familiar over the years. Some will be entirely unfamiliar to readers. An example of this phenomenon is the current lack of recognition of Asia's own brother Edwin. An actor as acclaimed in his time as the most popular movie star today, Edwin needed no introduction in 1874. Yet today blank stares would be the response to a mention of Edwin Booth in a college classroom.

Equally new and important in this edition is the opportunity to do justice to the author. Asia was never properly introduced in the Farjeon volume. The book was her own recollection, yet her identity and motive seemed ill-defined. What she said was clear, but not always who she was or why she said it. The preceding brief biography explains more fully the personal history of the author and the circumstances under which her remarkable memoir was written. The added information on her stormy marriage to Clarke throws light on the memoir's history.

It is important to remember in reading the account that it is not a traditional biography, not even in the nineteenth-century sense. There were large parts of her brother's life about which Asia knew and wrote little. Even the parts she knew well were difficult to relate in detail because family records had been so scattered. "All written or printed material found in our possession [in 1865], everything that bore his name was given up" to the authorites, she wrote in her memoir. "Not a vestige remains of aught that belonged to him." Unaided by such necessary sources, Asia was compelled to write from memory and from a few materials she had taken to Europe with her.

Several words of caution should be given. Asia is the sole source for much of what she gives us. No contemporary editor ever challenged the statements in her manuscript. It is prudent, therefore, to ask how reliable a reporter she is and how good a job she does in separating her own feelings from those she ascribes to her brother. Historians have been satisfied generally with her truthfulness. Common sense, however, demands caution in accepting lengthy word-for-word conversations, presented in quotation marks as direct statements yet pulled from memory after ten, fifteen, or even twenty years. These may capture the sense and passion of a moment but cannot be a verbatim record of it. Occasional errors of fact appear also. Asia would have known that it was at the Charles Street Theatre in her hometown of Baltimore where her brother first performed, not the St. Charles Theatre as she writes. The latter was a theater in New Orleans, forever notable in her mind as the site of her father's last performances before his sudden death. Such small errors, whether due to oversight or misinformation, might have been caught in her lifetime had a routine prepublication review of her manuscript been made. Where apparent, these mistakes have now been noted. Brief explanatory notes have been added in this edition where useful, and a small amount of text reorganization has furthered the goal of clarity. Asia's fondness for dashes, commas, and semicolons has also necessitated selective changes in punctuation where they make clear the meaning or reading of the text.

Beyond these few changes the memoir comes to us just as Asia wrote it. Modern readers will wince at her insulting racial language and the assumptions behind it. Others will be offended by her ethnic and class prejudices. Still others will wonder at her occasionally awkward phrases. But such was our author. Asia gave us no polished text, properly vetted for the reader by literary friends and a vigilant publisher. She left instead an intense and intimate conversation, thrown out unrefined from a sister's heart.

NOTES

1. Asia B. Clarke, *The Elder and The Younger Booth* (Boston: James R. Osgood, 1882), pp. 95–96.

2. Stephen M. Archer, *Junius Brutus Booth: Theatrical Prometheus* (Carbondale and Edwardsville: Southern Illinois University Press, 1992), chapters 5, 6.

3. Archer, p. 171.

4. Eleanor Ruggles, *Prince of Players, Edwin Booth* (N.Y.: W.W. Norton, 1953), p. 339.

5. *Baltimore American and Commercial Advertiser*, Sept. 27, 1899.

6. E. H. Bell, "Mr. J. S. Clarke," in Brander Matthews and Laurence Hutton, eds., *Actors and Actresses of Great Britain and the United States*, vol. 5 (New York: Cassell, 1886), p. 99.

7. Asia B. Clarke, *Personal Recollections of the Elder Booth* (London: privately printed, n.d.), p. 1.

8. Letter to Jean Anderson [Tudor Hall], Sept. 10, 1856. This is one of a number of letters from Asia to Jean Anderson located in collection ML518 at the Peale Museum, Baltimore, Maryland. All quotations attributed to Asia in this introduction are taken from this collection unless otherwise indicated.

9. Stanley Kimmel, *The Mad Booths of Maryland* (New York: Bobbs-Merrill, 1940), p. 375

10. *New York Mercury*, Sept. 20, 1884.

11. Ella V. Mahoney, *Sketches of Tudor Hall and the Booth Family* (Bel Air: author, 1931), p. 60.

12. Memoir, Farjeon edition, p. 19.

13. Memoir, p. 90.

14. Clarke, *The Elder and The Younger Booth*, pp. 106–107.

15. Dorothy Fox, "Home of an American Arch Villain," *Civil War Times Illustrated*, vol. 29 (March-April, 1990), p. 12.

16. Memoir, p. 96.

17. "The First Appearance of Two Famous Actors," undated clipping, Booth files, Harvard Theatre Collection.

18. *New York Mercury*, Sept. 20, 1884.

19. L. Terry Oggel, ed., *The Letters and Notebooks of Mary Devlin Booth* (New York and Westport: Greenwood Press, 1987), p. 37.

20. Memoir, p. 79; *New York Clipper*, May 7, 1859.

21. Biographical sketches of Clarke may be found conveniently in both the *Dictionary of American Biography* and the *Dictionary of National Biography*.

22. *New York Daily Tribune*, Sept. 26, 1899.

23. *New York Clipper*, April 20, 1861.

24. *Philadelphia Evening Bulletin*, Sept. 26, 1899.

25. *Elder and Younger Booth*, p. 158.

26. March 9, 1878.

27. A. K. McClure, *Recollections of Half a Century* (Salem, Mass.: Salem Press, 1902), p. 247.

28. Junius B. Booth to Edwin Booth, Philadelphia [April 24, 1865], Hampden-Booth Theatre Library, The Players, New York. The letter is reproduced in the section of family letters and documents.

29. "Affidavit of John S. Clarke," Washington, D.C., May 6, 1865. Investigation and Trial Papers Relating to the Assassination of President Lincoln, National Archives, M-599, reel 7, frames 0408–0412. The complete affidavit is reproduced in the section of family letters and documents.

30. Gene Smith, *American Gothic: The Story of America's Legendary Theatrical Family —Junius, Edwin, and John Wilkes Booth* (New York: Simon & Schuster, 1992), pp. 102–103.

31. Millward to Attorney General James Speed, Washington, April 25, 1865, Letters Received Series, 1809–70, Records of the Attorney General's Office, General Records of the Department of Justice, RG 60, National Archives, Archives II, College Park, Maryland.

32. Asia's memoir provides details of these events.

33. Clarke's statement of May 6, 1865, cited in note 29 (above).

34. See Junius's 1865 diary entries, reproduced in part in the family documents section.

35. Book 311-A, Old Capitol Prison Records, Department of Washington, Records of the Army Continental Commands, RG 393, National Archives, Washington, D. C.

36. *Personal Recollections of the Elder Booth*, pp. 20–22.

37. Preface, p. *viii*.

38. Copies of church records, shared by the late John C. Brennan, give the birth and baptismal dates for Asia's first six children (excepting Edwin Booth Clarke).

39. *New York Clipper*, May 26, 1888.

40. Identified in Asia's letter to Jean written from Brighton, England, February 12, 1871.

41. *New York Times*, March 19, 1868.

42. *New York Clipper,* June 18, 1870, quoting London's *Court Circular.*

43. New Series, vol. 6 (Sept. 1, 1885), p. 167.

44. E. H. Sothern, *The Melancholy Tale of "Me"* (New York: Charles Scribner's Sons, 1918), p. 93.

45. *New York Telegram,* June 10, 1895.

46. *Recollections of Half a Century,* p. 248.

47. *Boston Sunday Herald,* December 29, 1901.

48. Asia to Edwin Booth, July 14, 1879. Asia's letters to Edwin are quoted with permission of the Hampden-Booth Library, The Players.

49. Letter at the Hampden-Booth Library, The Players.

50. Laurence Hutton to Asia B. Clarke, New York, June 22, 1881, Hutton Letterbooks, vol. 14, Laurence Hutton Collection, Princeton University Library.

51. Asia B. Clarke to Edwin Booth, June 3, 1879, Hampden-Booth Library, The Players.

52. *New York Dramatic News,* April 6, 1878.

53. *The Era Almanack, 1883* (London: Era, n.d.), p. 73.

54. Obituary notices in her file at the Harvard Theatre Collection.

55. *Baltimore Sun,* June 2, 1888; records of Green Mount Cemetery, Baltimore, Md.

56. The close study given the manuscript by Arthur Kincaid and published by him in "The Unlocked Book Revisited," *Surratt Courier,* vol. 16 (September 1991), pp. 3–5, has been most useful.

57. For Eleanor Farjeon's account of her family's association with the manuscript, see *The Unlocked Book* (New York: G. P. Putnam's Sons, 1938), pp. 11–26.

MEMOIR

BY ASIA BOOTH CLARKE

John Wilkes was the ninth of ten children born to Junius Brutus and Mary Anne Booth. His birthplace was the Maryland [family] farm, twenty-five or twenty-eight miles from Baltimore city, and the date of his birth was the tenth of May 1838.

His mother, when he was a babe of six months old, had a vision, in answer to a fervent prayer, in which she imagined that the foreshadowing of his fate had been revealed to her. And as this incident was more painfully impressed upon her mind by a dream when he had attained manhood, both vision and dream were familiarized to me by frequent repetition. This is one of the numerous coincidences which tend to lead one to believe that human lives are swayed by the supernatural. Crediting it, we almost might accept undoubtedly those weird lines of Hood's:

> All of our acts of life are pre-ordained,
> And each pre-acted in their several spheres
> By ghostly duplicates.
> They sway our deeds by their performance.

The oft-told reminiscence was put into [the following] form and presented to the mother on her birthday. The lines claim no other merit than affording an explanation of her vision:

THE MOTHER'S VISION

Written 1854, June 2nd, by A[sia] B[ooth], Harford Co., Md.

> 'Tween the passing night and the coming day
> When all the house in slumber lay,

A patient mother sat low near the fire,
With that strength even nature cannot tire,
Nursing her fretful babe to sleep—
Only the angels these records keep
*   Of mysterious Love!*

One little confiding hand lay spread
Like a white-oped lily, on that soft fair bed,
The mother's bosom, drawing strength
and contentment warm—
The fleecy head rests on her circling arm.
In her eager worship, her fearful care,
Riseth to heaven a wild, mute prayer
*   Of foreboding Love!*

Tiny, innocent white baby-hand,
What force, what power is at your command,
For evil, or good? Be slow or be sure,
Firm to resist, to pursue, to endure—
My God, let me see what this hand shall do
In the silent years we are tending to;
*   In my hungering Love,*

I implore to know on this ghostly night
Whether 'twill labour for wrong, or right,
For—or against Thee?
*   The flame up-leapt*
Like a wave of blood, an avenging arm crept
Into shape; and **Country** *shown out in the*
*   flame,*
Which fading resolved to her boy's own name!
God had answered Love—
*   Impatient Love!*

The early schooldays of my brothers and self were passed
together under the same mistress, afterwards continued under

the same master.* John Wilkes was not quick at acquiring knowledge. He had to plod, progress slowly step by step, but that which he once attained he never lost. He found it far from easy to keep up with his classmates, but when the monthly review came he had not to re-study like the rest. What he had once learned remained, as he said, *stamped on the sight of his mind*, for he not only recollected, but saw it, so as to be able to turn to the part of the page immediately. He possessed a tenacious rather than an intuitive intelligence like his brothers. If he failed to compass a subject with such ease, at least he brought greater application and more energy to his work than they. He had great power of concentration, and he never let go a subject once broached until he had mastered it or proved its barrenness. From early boyhood he was argumentative and fervid in debate. At school he sat at his task with forehead clasped by both hands, mouth firm set, as if resolute to conquer.

He had a singular way of surmounting a difficulty. This was by individualizing his task or his work. He would imagine a column of spelling so many foes in line, and attacked them with a vigor which he declared nothing else could inspire. As for his sums, "Arithmetic," he said, was "amusement for *great* brains—it nearly drives me mad, but I'll not be beaten by dumb signs. When I set them up as battalions I always come out in victory."

In the same peculiar habit he pursued whatever work he had to do. After having read *The Pilgrim's Progress*, he said, "Bunyan understood exactly how small minds would grasp the abstract ideas when portrayed as men and women, and how to simplify his imaginative flights by familiar scenery, hill-climbing, and sinking into sloughs. Now, I understand Bunyan; he wrote for dullards like me." (And yet I have heard intelligent and well-read people declare they could not understand *The*

---

*Susan Hyde and Martin J. Kerney.

Pilgrim's Progress.) "When I want to do something that I know is wrong, or that I haven't time for, no surer way of being rid of the temptation than just to pretend it a *reality*, in form and life; and then I lay my demon."

This quality of combativeness was mostly directed against inanimate objects. It did not lead him to join any of the mock skirmishes or fighters of our little neighborhood, who for want of military discipline enrolled themselves under a twelve-year-old leader, and gloried in the title of "Bully Boys of Baltimore," trying their strength and determination in spoiling the childish beauty of each other's faces.

In committing to memory passages of Byron's *Giaour* he was so laughably persistent in the task that the house-hold became familiar with passages of the poem; yet he had not forgotten a word when, years later, he was called upon to recite them, for in the interim they had lain fast locked in memory. His was not, then, that quickly receptive mind, so enviable to pupils and masters, but, slow and steady, his well-balanced brain comprehended and applied what it had acquired. The consequence was a remarkable retentiveness, but to this careful precision of mental quality, had sluggish and deliberate feelings been allied, the result must have been a cool-headed and coldhearted individuality. On the contrary, his feelings were ardent and impulsive; in a moment of devotion or enthusiasm he would grant or give anything he possessed, while in time of danger his quick eye took in the situation regardless of his own safety. His coolness and self-poise commanded confidence. He was never known to throw off a friend or to slight an acquaintance; the loves of his boyhood were those of his manhood; his affection was as retentive as his memory.

One summer evening when the streets were dusky, and the inhabitants seated, as was customary in our city, on their doorsteps and porches in the cool air, a crowd of young people were engaged in playing "telegraph." This was a firework line stretched from one neighbor's tree to that of another across the road. The line had carried the firework successfully, sent in turn by six or seven different boys, when Wilkes' turn came. He fixed the wire to one of our maples, and to the paper-mulberry tree opposite; a man had unobserved walked under it, and his hat was caught. He called out angrily, but without showing much annoyance, and disappeared. As the telegraph was fired, and Wilkes was about unfastening the wire from the maple, a constable caught his shoulder; he had approached silently from the opposite direction, accompanied by the man whose hat had been treated ignominiously. Youth of both sexes mysteriously vanished, and Wilkes said, "Just let me coil up the wire, officer, or we'll have a horse's head off—that'll be worse than a man's hat, won't it?"

Down those silent streets no vehicle or horses passed in the evening hours, and no foot passengers ever behaved so eccentrically as to promenade on the rough cobblestones. We heard the words, "To the Watch-house," and Wilkes said quickly, "Don't frighten mother; I'll go all right."

He walked away with the constable, who was in the ordinary citizen dress of the day, and I hastily ran on before to a friend's house and asked the master of it to come with us. He promised to follow quickly and leaving him to do so, I tied my little silk apron over my head for a bandanna, and joined the two who came walking leisurely along. The constable had not his hand upon my brother, and linking my arm in his we went through several narrow by-ways to the old Watch-house. We mounted an ill-looking staircase and entered a dim filthy room, stifling with bad odors and heat. On a raised form behind a railing sat three formidable men. Notwithstanding their linen coats half off their backs, their open shirt fronts and limp collars, they presented a terrible array, for they were mighty men of the law. A few dim candles were guttering in the unwholesome air, and the dreaded official called out at once, "Let's hear what these children have done, and get them out of this smothering place."

The accuser, with the hat which had suffered ill-treatment, stood forward, as my brother, removing his low cap from his head, answered respectfully and promptly the questions put to him. He never once looked towards the man who was wronged, but kept his gaze upon the magistrate. The accuser was excited, and inclined to be severe; he had to be calmed down repeatedly by the constable, who said gruffly, "Silence, can't ye?"

Then Wilkes was asked to give up the names of his mates. "*Must* I do that?" he asked.

The magistrate began slowly, "Well, yes, unless you . . ."

"Then I refuse to give their names."

"Honor among thieves," shouted the angry accuser.

"Silence!" a sharp voice growled, while the magistrate pursued, "How is it only you were caught? For this gentleman declares there were a dozen of you boys."

The audacious victim, to my horror, dared to smile at me. "Because that is my luck, sir, I guess."

I had been so annoyed that he had not given the names of his comrades who had run away from him, that, seizing this opportunity, I spoke hurriedly. "No matter what game or mischief it is, *he* always fares worse than the others. *He* is the one to be hurt or found out, and all the rest get off clear. And he's not a bit worse than they."

The magistrate took no notice of my defense, but I was sure the voice came from him that said: "Not half so bad, *you* think."

The fine was settled, and Mr. C. Cole*, our friend, stepped forward and paid the money, giving his name and profession, both of which seemed to be held in esteem. After a few words of warning about "obstructing the pass-way" to Wilkes, and a kindly smile at me, the magistrate said, "Now, you children, go straight home."

Our mother had only heard of the occurrence as we were approaching her door. Before the excitement was over we were

---

*Cornelius M. Cole, clerk of the city commissioners.

told that Mr. O'Laughlin* had had a piece of percussion cap fired into his cheek. It was permissible for young people to play with miniature cannon and firearms in those patriotic days, and this accident had occurred in play. Wilkes tried to extract the bit of copper with a needle, but turning ill, would have fainted had he not been placed immediately in the air, and the operation was deftly performed by a feminine hand, which probed deep for the jagged bit of copper. It may be that this cardinal virtue of Fortitude is more essentially a feminine quality, for many courageous men have been known to shrink from the sight of a bloodless operation even, and the boy who could stand unflinchingly before a magistrate holding unknown terrors locked in every slowly uttered word was certainly courageous, although in less than a half-hour afterward he succumbed at sight of his friend's pain.

John Wilkes was placed at a large boarding school kept by Quakers, in a Quaker settlement at Cockeysville. His father was desirous of purchasing a farm in that vicinity in order to provide a home and occupation for his two younger sons, when they should have completed their school life. After having visited the place several times, his ardor somewhat abated when he discovered that there was no thoroughfare or right of way to the farm, the path then used for access being only permitted through the courtesy of a neighbor. Mr. Booth gave up the idea of securing this, to his mind, "desirable piece of property," and kindly presented the conveyancer with a sum of money to requite him for his attention and loss of time. This unbusinesslike way of dealing with a business man led to an unpleasant difficulty and a threatened lawsuit after the decease of Mr. Booth, as the conveyancer declared that "he accepted the money as a retaining fee." The case was satisfactorily adjusted by the family lawyer, Mr. Sleigh, and the sons were left unprovided for at the death of their father.

---

*Apparently not the father of Michael O'Laughlen; he died in 1843.

His monetary affairs, as far as his children were concerned, were pitiable failures; and by trusting to the honor and probity of others, his wealth, except that which was settled upon our mother, was easily diverted into other channels.

This digression is merely to show that his sons made their own way in life unassisted.

The Quaker school, although extensive, and commanding a charming view of country, never assumed any title more imposing than that of "the school."* It was conducted by a family named Lamb, and the gentleness of the inmates of that solid stone mansion was communicated to even the boys with lupine propensities who entered their home-like circle. My mother and myself were invited to a picnic at the breaking-up of school. We went by train to Cockeysville and were unceremoniously deposited with a carload of other guests on a perilously narrow platform at the edge of a broken road. The shriek of the locomotive had died away before we discovered a great high-crowned white-covered wagon, drawn by oxen, approaching. A merry boy, dressed in white shirt and white trousers, with a broad straw flapping hat, and a narrow strip of blue ribbon at his throat, hailed us, "Will thee jump down, and come to wagon — 'cus wagon can't get to *thee.*" He broke into a merry laugh, and as if apologizing for his daring wit, he added gravely, "Thee *sees* I can't get no nearer."

The jump was not easy for the elderly people, but it was accomplished amid much merriment and much conjuring of others "not to look." The boy with his spotless linen and blue ribbon, which was the only streak of color on the Grounds, except what the abundant flower beds and trellised vines displayed, was the servant, sent to transport us to the woods. He addressed all the young gentlemen boarders by their pet names, or abbreviated Christian names, unlike the custom of the Friends, who conscientiously give the full appellation

---

*An error. The academy was known as the Milton Boarding School, run by John E. Lamb (1803–1885), Quaker educator.

as pronounced at baptism. I was startled by hearing this boy exclaim, "Here comes Sam, miss. It's for thee—the horse." One of our youthful Baltimore friends came dashing up on a great white horse. S. Sutton*, the heralded Sam, had been deputed as advance-courier to inform the guests that a vehicle was coming for their accommodation, but as the guests, male and female, were seating themselves on the floor of the great wagon, in the clean deep straw, the handsome fellow insisted on me mounting before him in the saddle.

"What—in snowy white, and in a Quaker settlement? Children!" exclaimed my mother, in an unmistakably negative tone.

My mother had been particular that our dresses should not be conspicuous in the company we were to mingle with, so that I was dressed in white, bonnet, and flowers, "and all," while she wore lilacs and a dress of pale grey. On the Ground, which was under cover of great trees, we were greeted by hosts of pleasant Friends. The much talked of Ground was very uneven and broken. In fact, we had seen nothing but dense woodland, tall trees, and thick underbrush, the railroad seemed only a broad ribbon dividing a wood. It reminded me of the sorrowful and indignant criticism of a little town-bred darkie whom I had once taken to our own old farm-home.

"Well, Bill, this is the country at last."

"*Country!*" he sneered, with a contemptuous look around and upward. "Don't see no *country!* Sees nuffin' but everlastin' *trees*."

Tables of great length, and seating three hundred people, were constructed in these shadowy places. They were soon plenteously filled, and presided over by every one, without distinction. The females were all pretty, even the plain-faced were beautified by the grace of simplicity, and kindness seemed to be of their nature. The Elder, a benign and holy-looking man, very bent and aged, was placed with much show of affection

---

*A neighbor from Exeter Street.

in the midmost seat, and the pleasant women, wearing their plain lisse caps and their modest kerchiefs across their breasts, were as delighted as the broad-brimmed brethren to see him among them.

The lovely weather, the excellent dinner, and the cheery, unaffected hospitality of those assembled, rendered this a gala day long to be remembered. On the conclusion of the repast, of which servants, farm laborers, and stablemen partook side by side with guests and employers, a long unbroken silence fell. It was maintained until the Elder spoke, and it recalled the old nursery superstition—that he who first breaks a silence by speech has felt the passing over of an angel's wing. The entire band of old and young made their way, as requested, to a space beyond, where a stage had been erected. The benches were hurriedly carried and arranged for the accommodation of the spectators and the distribution of prizes, and verbal commendation for those who had industriously striven were made. Then followed recitations, and a lad of twelve or fourteen years of age leaped on the stage and astonished us with Othello's declamation. When we had recovered from the surprise of his gladiator-like entrance, we certainly could not withhold our applause, for he had an excellent voice, and spoke out like an actor. Wilkes stood near, watching his classmate with a nervous pale face. The reason was obvious when, after a pause, Wilkes himself came upon the little stage with all the fury of old Shylock.

"I say my daughter is my flesh and blood!"

A master, who stood screened by the boys nearest the platform, read out Salarino's, the servant's, and Tubal's lines, and Shylock had the stage to himself. The storm of passion, the lull of despair, the wild hysterical rejoicing—"I am very glad of it. I'll plague him, I'll torture him, I am glad of it"—were most earnestly given, and the doleful murmur of torture at the loss of the turquoise, "I had it of Leah when I was a bachelor," and with that dreary shaking of the head, as more remembering departed days than grieving for his loved jewel—

"I would not have given it for a whole wilderness of monkeys!" was provocative of a sadness which was rudely dispersed by his venomous tirade—"I'll have the heart of him if he forfeit!"

The general impression created by this scene was visible in each countenance, and in the stillness which followed the wild exit of Shylock. A swift torrent of applause recalled the young actor, who smiled, and blushed, and bowed repeatedly. A Quakeress beside me said, "What is his name? He is a comely youth. Does thee think we are as merciful to the Hebrews as we should be? They are a benighted race, and we are permitted to enjoy so many privileges and blessings denied to them."

Does thee think? Oh, what could *I* know about the rights of nations, what did I care for any other Hebrew than the one who was tugging at my dress-sleeve, to "get away from thee and thou, and meet me over there in the hollow. I've something to tell." I met Wilkes in the hollow forthwith, and throwing himself along the ground, he leaned his head back against my knees and said, "It is this." Unfolding a strip of paper from his pocket, he read what he called "his fortune," which a Gipsey prowling hereabouts had told him a few days since.*

"See here," he said, "I've written it, but there was no need to do that, for it is so bad that I shall not soon forget it."

The paper is ragged thro' much folding, and the boyish pencil writing is worn away. It was only a Gipsey's tattle for money, but who shall say there is no truth in it?

"Ah, you've a bad hand; the lines all cris-cras. It's full enough of sorrow. Full of trouble. Trouble in plenty, everywhere I look. You'll break hearts, they'll be nothing to you. You'll die young, and leave many to mourn you, many to love you too, but you'll be rich, generous, and free with your money. You're born under an unlucky star. You've got in your hand a thundering crowd of enemies—not one friend—you'll make a bad end, and have plenty to love you afterwards. You'll have a fast life—short, but

---

*Newspapers had reported the presence of English gypsies in parts of Maryland in 1851.

a grand one. Now, young sir, I've never seen a worse hand, and I wish I hadn't seen it, but every word I've told is true by the signs. You'd best turn a missionary or a priest and try to escape it."

"I asked her," Wilkes said, as he slowly refolded the paper, "'if it's in the stars, or in my hand, which is the same thing to you. How am I to escape it? It's a good thing that it is so short, as it is so bad a fortune. For this evil dose do you expect me to cross your palm?' She took her money though and said that she was glad she was not a young girl, or she'd follow me through the world for my handsome face."

He laughed at this, but the fortune had not ceased to trouble him, and at intervals, through the course of the few years that summed his life, frequent recurrence was sadly made to the rambling words of that old Gipsey in the wood of Cockeysville. This seed of an inherent superstition was kept alive by early association with the negroes, whose fund of ghost stories, legends, and ill omens never knew exhaustion.

The leader of the orchestra at one of the theaters in Baltimore gave Wilkes lessons on the flute, and a Mr. J. R. Codet[*], a stage dancer who was of so small a stature and slight build that he was frequently engaged to play the Duke of York in *Richard the Third* with the elder Booth, was the dancing master who gave Wilkes lessons in the Highland Fling, Sailor's Hornpipe, and a difficult Polish dance. This was to give grace and ease of deportment. He was square-shouldered and finely formed, but with that erect commanding bearing which would well suit Roman characters, not the princely gait or repose of Hamlet, nor the dashing agility of Petruchio.

Himself and younger brother were placed at the finishing school at Catonsville, St. Timothy's Hall, under the tutelage of Messrs. Van Bockelen and Guderdonk[†]. They here received

---

[*]Codet operated a "dancing academy" on Lombard Street in the late 1840s.
[†]Libertus Van Bokkelen (1815–1889) and Henry Onderdonk (1822–1895), Episcopalian priests.

Baptism*, and were prepared for the Confirmation according to the Episcopal Church. They entered the Hall as artillery cadets, and wore the steel-grey uniform of the class. Some of the best names of Maryland were on the roll of students at this Hall, names that have resounded through our country both in honor and contumely, names, too, that seem to have gone down in silence with the cause they espoused.

There was a celebrated Indian Chief named Billy Bowlegs†, and Wilkes went by this name among his companions at Catonsville. As a boy he was beloved by his associates, and as a man few could withstand the fascination of his modest, gentle manners. He inherited some of the most prepossessing qualities of his father, and while that father's finely shaped head and beautiful face were reproduced in him, he had the black hair and large hazel eyes of his mother. These were fringed heavily with long up-curling lashes, a noticeable peculiarity as rare as beautiful. He had perfectly shaped hands, and across the back of one he had clumsily marked, when a little boy, his initials in India ink.

One great charm of his attractiveness was the fact of his being a good listener. This is an accomplishment perhaps, but it is perfected only by the help of an unselfish and charitable disposition. It may too be badly assumed by a wily or shrewd person, but in Wilkes a certain deference and reverence towards his superiors in authority and age were very winning. With patience and respect he would listen to the most annoying people, sit calmly through the most aggravating relation of inane talkers, but when his turn came he would wear his argument threadbare. His discussion was didactic, if not always interesting, yet his conceit was never so great that he refused correction. The oratorical powers of the cadets of St. Timothy's were, without doubt, encouraged and cultivated.

---

*John Wilkes and Joseph Booth were baptized at St. Timothy's Episcopal Church in Catonsville on January 23, 1853.

†Billy Bowlegs (1810–1864), Seminole leader.

Stump-speaking was the delight of those youths who longed to make their voices heard throughout the country. It was almost a bad school for fostering that wild ambition born in Wilkes Booth and fed to fever-heat by the unhealthy tales of Bulwer*.

For some hardship, real or imaginary, the boys of St. Timothy's rebelled against their masters and withdrew to the woods, defying authority and restraint. The fathers of several of the boys were sent for and were for a long time powerless to effect reconciliation.

A letter came from Wilkes saying "Something is rotten in the state of Denmark." "Foul meat, eaten with silver forks." "All that glitters is not gold."

The boys had desired a change of diet, and were deprived of some holiday on account of their refusal to eat the food provided for them. They revenged themselves by slaughtering a number of chickens, then openly rebelled and camped in the woods.

After the death and burial of our father we were removed to the country home where the delightful summer vacations had been passed during the years of school-life. We could now talk of the days when we used to play "Christopher Columbus," which was by following the innumerable little brooks that intersected part of the land, and by the aid of our long poles leaping from stone to stone until, arriving on terra firma with a great shout, we planted the cross. We remembered, as some time long gone, when we had dug for Indian remains, confidently hoping to discover a skeleton intact or a bag full of bones. The exciting wish gave us fresh courage to use the spade and pick, and the long cavern we made we called our trench. Now, however, the two brothers resolved to become farmers, and they obtained a reluctant consent to clear a strip of woodland near the main road in order to erect a hut, where they could rest and refresh themselves after work.

---

*Edward Bulwer-Lytton (1803-1873), English novelist of popular melodramatic works.

The felling of trees for this hut was the first departure from the established rules [of the father against cutting trees] so long adhered to. All day the sound of their axes was heard, and tired out they came home to rest, oftentimes too exhausted to bathe or to eat, for like inexperienced workmen they did not husband their strength, but expended it excitedly. The hut was planned and some foundation logs laid, when a discussion arose about the position of the door. Each member of the family volunteered advice on the subject. Wilkes wanted the door open and facing the road, so that passers-by might see into their cozy habitation and be seen by them. His brother argued that there were seldom any persons passing on that road, and wanted the door to face the setting sun, which was the only time-teller at the farm. They started to work again, still undecided about the door, and returned to the house late in the afternoon. They had disturbed a hornet's nest and presented a pitiable sight, for their faces were swollen and disfigured, their eyes blackened and scarcely visible. One of the black women ran off to the stream for a shovel-full of branch mud, with which we daubed their faces, and after great resistance they were both made to swallow a dose of castor oil. They submitted to the disagreeable application of black mud, and by noon of the following day their watery and blood-shotten eyes were visible. Quite willingly at their mother's request they abandoned all idea of completing the hut, and Joseph Booth very soon afterward went to a boarding school at Easton or Elkton[*], while Wilkes prepared to engage "extra hands" to assist the blacks and himself, for he superintended the work in the coming harvest time.

A year had elapsed before the astounding revelation was made, with much laughter and ridicule, that when they were building that hut, not satisfied where to place the door, high words ensued, which led to disagreement and to blows. Then

---

[*]In an 1854 letter Asia states that Joe was attending school in Elkton, Cecil County, Md.

the two had fought until both were exhausted, and neither had conquered. It was a furious contest, and being equally matched, there showed no hope of victory on either side until, strength failing completely, both gave in and agreed upon a lie to hide their disgrace. Each brother declared that he held a higher opinion of the other's prowess after the fight. The dangerous hornets which infested the place presented a laudable excuse for them, and it is well known how those vicious little creatures attack the eyes of their disturbers. It was somewhat satisfactory to reflect how unremittingly we had applied those mud bandages and how resolutely we had poured down their wicked throats those doses of castor oil.

The first evidence of an undemocratic feeling in Wilkes was shown when we were expected to sit down with our hired workmen. It was the custom for members of the family to dine and sup with the white men who did the harvesting. Wilkes had a struggle with his pride and knew not which to abide by, his love of equality and brotherhood, or that southern reservation which jealously kept the white laborer from free association with his employer or his superior. His father would not have hesitated an instant, nor would Richard Booth, the rebel-patriot grandfather, have considered the matter twice. The difference between the impassioned self-made Republican and the native-born southern American is wide. One overleaps restraint by his enthusiasm, desiring to cast off at a swoop the trammels of a former allegiance, and is over eager to fraternize with all men; but the other cautiously creates for himself a barrier called respect, with which he fences off familiarity and its concomitant evils. This made the master a god in the South, to be either loved or feared. There were no "Masters" and "Mistresses" in the North. No northerner would be so rash as to hint at the assumption of such a title, even while yearning for the distinction. Thus they unwillingly yielded, and forced themselves to encourage undue familiarity with those, too often the refuse of other countries, who had been in more servile bondage than the American slaves. Often grating under the insolent freedom of these ignorant menials whom they dared not even to call *servants*, northern women vaunted their love of equality and called themselves democratic.

Wilkes made a compromise with his pride, as he termed it, and desired us, his mother and sisters, not to be present at the meals with the men, while he sat at the side of his table, giving the head to the oldest workman. The honor was kindly acknowledged, but inquiry began to be made for the "ladies," whose lack of attendance was fitly excused at each meal. However, at the last dinner one young fellow asked, "If the ladies thought theirselves too mighty good to eat with us 'hands'? I only asked for information," he added, "because at the house of one of them big bugs, the Fernandez*, who calls theirselves related somehow to Pokyhontas—whoever that blamed creetur is—the *lady-folk* were never seen at *our* table, so we took dudgeon, and jest writ our 'pinion of such conduct on their nice white tablecloth with their best strawberry and lemon jam."

"Oh, don't bother us about women," Wilkes interrupted quickly, "drink your cider, and, Stonebreaker, give us 'Ben Bolt'† in your heaviest style."

Songs went round after this innovation, and the party strayed off for the short midday nap under the trees before resuming work.

Sons of the soil in the scantiest of clothing, with the sweat of honest labor on their sunbeat faces, with voracious appetites that seemed hungering in the midst of rapid gratification, after the "plug" of tobacco laid carefully beside their "chunk" of bread, were not the most delightsome guests to entertain, particularly in a hot kitchen in the scorching days of August. But these men, mostly natives of foreign lands, where the gulf is impassable between the high and the lowly, are on this side of the ocean invariably the severest and most punctilious clients of what they miscall Liberty. We were not a popular family with our white laborers, because, as they said, "They'd heer'd

---

*Henry D. Farnandis (1817–1890), wealthy state senator, businessman, and corporation lawyer.

†"Ben Bolt," a popular ballad of the 1840s.

we had dirty British blood, and being mixed up with Southern ideas and niggers made it dirtier."

This was the first attempt at hiring white labor, and the next proved almost as unpleasant. Even as young and inexperienced in these vexed questions as we were, still we observed enough to let us understand that grommelling of disaffection which would ultimately drive out black labor.

Wilkes one day was lamenting his lack of grace and said that he was "jerky and stiff and too awkward for the stage." Besides, he complained; "How shall I ever have a chance on the stage? Buried here, torturing the grain out of the ground for daily bread, what chance have I of ever studying elocution or declamation?"

He found an old book of his father's and tried to learn, from its signs, the inflection and guidance of the voice. We carefully read together *Dr. Rush on the Voice**, but concluded that little could be effected without a master. On several occasions he dressed himself in a petticoat and draped a shawl around him for a toga. Then he put on my long-trained dress and walked before the long glass, declaring that he would succeed as Lady Macbeth in the sleep-walking scene. He secretly "got himself up" after Charlotte Cushman as Meg Merrilees†, and terrified me and all the darkies, who shrieked, "Ondress Mars' Johnnie, ondress him!" As for the elocution, he practiced every day in the woods, letting his deep strident tones die away in echoes, now soft and mellow, then wildly fierce and charged with passion, but whether wrong or right, by rule or emphasis, neither he nor I could tell. I only knew what I told him, that his voice was a beautiful organ, with perfect music in it. It needed the master to prune, cultivate, subdue, and encourage.

---

*Dr. James Rush (1786–1869), author of *The Philosophy of the Human Voice* (1827) and a friend of the elder Booth.

†Charlotte Cushman (1816–1876), actor whose roles included the gypsy-like Meg Merrilies in the play *Guy Mannering*.

I was a better judge of ease and deportment, and dressed in my skirts, with a little scarf held over his shoulders, he walked the room before the mirror, becoming more and more charmed with himself. He said merrily, "I'll walk across the fields yonder, to see if the darkies can discover me."

He put on the tiny bonnet then in fashion, and went out across the fields. The men took off their hats, as they paused in their work to salute him. He passed on to the barn, where he was greeted in the same respectful manner, and came back to the house delighted with his success, which he attributed to his "elegant deportment."

His disposition was cheerful and gay, but he was a singular combination of gravity and joy. The songs he loved, and he was passionately fond of music, were all sad and plaintive ones. He could understand the sadness in the jews' harp of the darky twanging out a tuneless noise in the dark kitchen, but to my mind resembling nothing so much as a great buzzing insect trying vainly to get at liberty, and the negro-made tunes in doleful minor, with the real improvised negro sentiment or fun, were eagerly sought by him. He was full of merriment too, but hated jokes, particularly theatrical ones. He used to say to a prosy narrator of worn-out stage anecdote, "Don't bring damnation on yourself by swearing to the truth of your anecdotes, let them off as jokes." And again, "I know these good old tales are only lies, but when you vouch for the truth of them so seriously, a fellow feels such a fool pretending he believes them, and trying to look surprised and to laugh always in the right place."

This plain speaking spoiled the flavor of many a pungent joke that had never fallen flat before.

"I cannot see why sensible people," said Wilkes, "will trouble themselves to concoct ridiculous stories of their great actors. *We* know that two-thirds of the funny anecdotes about our own father are disgraceful falsehoods. Now, for instance, that comical account of yours about the company finding him sitting on a rock in the Gunpowder River and having to fish him out in time to get ready to act Sir Edward Mortimer. We know well enough that our father never went for a day's fishing anywhere, and that he never plied a fishing rod in his life. I often wonder where the fun is, and where the merit lies, and who invented that preposterous lie of Mrs. Siddons stabbing the potato."*

The droll thoughtful way in which he uttered this concluding remark caused a burst of laughter, in which the snubbed anecdotarian joined, not unwillingly.

A friend of ours who was a man of letters and of great experience advised us conjointly to write the biography of our father. He intimated that soon some actor or newspaper-man would undertake the task without the conscientiousness with which we could give it. He strongly urged us without delay to set about collecting memoranda, old letters, playbills and criticisms, and offered to aid us in every possible way that he could. Very shortly after this, my mother had occasion to overlook the bookcases and old trunks that had lain locked since father's death, and with that morbid grief which imagines a life *ended for ever* because it is past to the mourner who survives, she deliberately seated herself to the task which awoke the bitterest indignation of myself and brother. We crouched near her on the floor, open-eyed and greedy for letters and information, while she read over and destroyed pile upon pile of letters. At a push from Wilkes, I ventured to speak, "Oh, Mother, give us some autographs—some old letters—for remembrance."

Then Wilkes, "Supposing someone should write father's life. You are leaving nothing to refer to. Such a lot of incorrect dates and false statements will be made. Give *us* the proofs, and everything that can be of service."

This was met by a decided repulse. The destruction by fire and fingers still went on. We sat watching the precious documents which our father had carefully kept tied in packets, and numbered precisely, increase the heap in the basket, and grim and ugly as Macbeth's witches, we growled inwardly at

---

*A celebrated story told of Sarah Siddons (1755–1831) to illustrate her lusty appetite.

this cruel and wanton destruction. At long intervals mother would pause and tear off a name from a letter, giving us in this way such autographs as Tom Flynn, Elliston, Cooper, Daddy Rice, etc., but the *letters* were doomed to smoke.

In more recent time, we heard how the dutiful daughter of John Wilkes the Englishman* carefully destroyed her father's papers, and every scrap of writing she could lay her irreverent hands upon, after his death. Wilkes declared this to be "homicidal mania," and we could ill conceal our just anger at the destruction of our father's papers. Our literary friend was as annoyed at our loss as we, but at the same time he could not refrain laughing when he saw our fallen countenances. We had gone to Baltimore with mother buoyant with such eager hopes, elated with the certainty of bringing back trunks full of playbills, old books, diaries and letters. As it was, we both worked earnestly at the biography, and by talking with our mother we were enabled to take down much information and correct data. Then we visited an old relative, who had hoards of precious theatrical books, and gleaned from him. We copied word for word [father's] diary of an early date, all the letters we could obtain, and a scrap of an old "part" on which was preserved his desire to obtain the post of lighthouse-keeper. We came also into possession of a few memoranda in father's own writing, and truly we delved and worked like moles in forgotten old corners and brought to light and order a rather large collection of interesting matter. This was the beginning, in difficulty and often in despair, of the "Memoir of the Elder Booth."

Wilkes' bedroom was facing the east. He said, "No setting sun view for me, it is too melancholy; let me see him rise." Which he frequently did, coming home from the hunt and the Know-Nothing meetings, which were held at some secret place several miles distant; or in busy times when he was compelled to set the men to work at sun-up. He wanted no carpet on his floor. He "liked the smell of the oak." A huge pair of antlers

---

*John Wilkes (1727–1797), radical English politician and reformer to whom the Booth family claimed kin.

held swords, pistols, daggers and a rusty old blunderbuss. A large case contained his school-books, small, cheaply-bound volumes of Bulwer, Maryatt, Byron, and a large Shakespeare, with Roman and Grecian histories, small volumes of Longfellow, Whittier, Milton, N. P. Willis, Poe, and Felicia Hemans' poems. These red-covered books had been purchased by himself or presented by young friends. His bed was the hardest mattress and a straw pillow, for at this time of his life he adored Agesilaus, the Spartan King, and disdained luxuries.[*]

In winter I threw over his bed a quilt that I had made of Job-tears pattern. "Oh, take away that sorrowful canopy," he said, pretending to shiver. "I shall always see old Job at the foot of my bed, naked and bent, with long white locks, and beard hanging to his knees, and shedding tears as big as these patches. I have seen a picture like that somewhere, and I don't want to be haunted and made melancholy by the thought of Job. I think God tried him to the very verge of despair."

Once he burst out with the joyous exclamation, "Heaven and Earth! how glorious it is to live! how divine! to breathe this breath of life with a clear mind and healthy lungs!" "Don't let us be sad," he would say. "Life is so short, and the world is so beautiful. Just to *breathe* is delicious."

Yet through all his fitful gaiety there was traceable a taint of melancholy, as if the shadow of his mother's vision or the Gypsey's fortune fell with his sunshine. Perhaps the forecast of his awful doom lay over him. In the woods he would throw himself face downward and nestle his nose close into the earth, taking long sniffs of the "earth's healthy breath," he called it. He declared this process of inhaling wholesome odors and rich scents was delightful, but could never induce me to try. He called it "burrowing," and he loved to nibble at sweet roots and twigs, so that I called him a rabbit. He was ardently fond of outdoor life, but was never a sportsman nor an angler. He was a lover of botany and geology, and many of the specimens

---

[*]Agesilaus, ascetic king of Sparta and one of its finest generals, 4th century B.C.

in my now limited collection are of his obtaining and selection. He was very tender of flowers, and of insects and butterflies. Lightning bugs he considered as "bearers of sacred torches," and would go out of his way to avoid injuring them. He once, after nights of endeavor, caught me a katy-did just to show me what the little nuisance was like. I wanted it eagerly for my collection.

"No you don't, you bloodthirsty female," he said, putting the creature in his breast. "Katy shall be free and shall sing tonight out in the sycamores." Then kissing the small thing, he said, "Oh you small devil. How you can banish sleep, quiet, and good temper! Katy, you fiend, how many nights you have kept me awake cursing your existence!" With that he walked over to the trees, and laid the little night brawler safely among the leaves, to tune her pipes for night once more.

Through the long drowsy days of summer, the long delightful evenings, in the dull winter time, we two were thrown much together. Joseph Booth passed the greater part of his time at boarding schools. Edwin and Junius were in California. My sister had been from childhood always more or less an invalid, and the mother buried herself in grief for her lost husband, and the settlement of her intricate affairs, for he had died without having left a will. Wilkes and I had many tastes in common; we both loved music and reading aloud, both preferred verse to prose. We went through many ponderous books together, read histories of other countries and of our own, *The Life of Algernon Sydney*, Plutarch's *Lives and Morals*, and Nathaniel Hawthorne. The rest were poems and light verse, which we generally reserved for outdoor reading. He played the flute and we sang together, accompanied by the piano or the guitar. He would recite poems and much of the play of *Julius Caesar*, and some other tragedies, while I held the book.

Jesse Wharton, an old schoolmate from Catonsville, was an ever welcome guest at our house.* He was a rarely en-

---

*Wharton, a southern sympathizer, was shot to death by a guard he provoked at the Old Capitol Prison in Washington in 1862.

dowed youth both physically and mentally. I sat listening one day to their astounding stories of schooldays, and Jesse said [to Wilkes], "Do you remember the day, Billy, that you were nearly drowned, sucked under by the current? I tell you," he continued, addressing himself to me, "our hearts stood still *that* time; we never thought to see this fellow open his big eyes again." At the moment of speaking thus, Jesse laid his arm affectionately around Wilkes' neck, who laid his cheek down upon his friend's hand as it rested upon his shoulder.

He said, drawing a long breath, "No, Jess, I am not to drown, hang, or burn, although my sister yonder has believed I am a predestined martyr of some sort, ever since the time when she sat the whole night through reading *Fox's Book of Martyrs.*"

This led to comparison of books they had read. There were no novels in those days within easy grasp of young people, if indeed there were such publications. All that *we* knew of were little pamphlets of Boz's bewildering English life, Sir Walter Scott and Bulwer. The two walked away to inspect Wilkes's unpretentious library in his own room. I could smell the tobacco of their pipes and hear their occasional laughter, while I sat wondering what they would both be in the far-off time. They were both so handsome, so gifted, and so light-hearted; for my brother, no visions or dreams were too extravagantly great for me to indulge; to all who knew him, his was a future so full of promise.

Wilkes had a beautiful black colt without a white hair or spot, a long silken mane and tail which I frequently used to braid in tiny plaits, he was so gentle and docile. He had an *Ivanhoe* forehead, on which was imprinted many a loving kiss by his master, who had broken him in himself and named him Cola di Rienzi.* Wilkes taught me to ride, with and without a saddle, to go through all the graceful maneuvers of a wild and daring horsewoman, and as he was a fearless rider, I kept by his side through many dangerous and isolated miles of country.

---

*A Roman patriot and hero of a novel by Bulwer (1835).

My proudest accomplishment was to lope or run while keeping a firm seat sideways on a man's saddle; as all men's saddles are military I could hold tight with my knee to the front, my toe in one stirrup, and never budge a half inch from the saddle. He would start Cola off with, "The Choctows are after you, ride for your life." And Cola, at least, seemed to believe it. Thus Cola learned many tricks of his master; to stamp for "No," and to neigh and bow for "Yes," to lie down as dead, and to follow obediently. One morning Wilkes went to the stable and his colt, as he was fondly designated even when decidedly in maturity, instead of nestling his head as usual to his master for a kiss, bit him viciously on the cheek.

Someone afterward noticing the cut, he made answer, "Cola bit me!" His lips quivered, and the tears came over his cheeks as he said, "I could have stood anything but that. I love the creature so. A kick or any fit of temper might be accounted for, but for a pet horse to turn and bite is *vicious.*"

We took early morning rides before sun-up, when the dew lay like rain on the grass, and evening rides by moonlight, singing aloud as we rode. It was on one of these quiet nights as we let our horses walk, while we enjoyed the pungent odors of the pines and the smoky scent of the Lombardy poplars after the fierce shower, that on emerging from the long archway of trees, Wilkes broke out into a gay song: "I love the merry, merry sunshine," and the horses started at a quickened pace in time with his singing. After that, letting the reins lay loosely on their necks, he sang first a slow sad tune, and, without a touch of ours, the animals fell into measure. Then we started a lively air, and they quickened their gait to our time. We frequently amused ourselves in this way; but on one portentous afternoon I announced a far more wonderful discovery.

"Another continent?" laughed he, hanging half in and half out of a hammock fashioned from a guano bag and ropes.

"No, come, quick as thought—frogs!"

I caught up the guitar and rushed off so excitedly to the woods, whence I had come disturbing his repose, that he was constrained to follow. We paused under the trees which hung over to the low hazels on the opposite side, of what we knew as the Hickory road, a narrow hilly lane rugged with gulches and large stones or rocks. It was an almost unused thoroughfare, and the great dense woods beyond were "no man's land." We were as much at home therein as on the other side of our own fences. We got silently over the fence and sat on a lovely knoll of yellow-starred moss, springy and soft as cushions. The stream, or rivulet rather, came gurgling under the fence and took its way across the road to the woods opposite, where it lost itself in tangled masses of wild-grape bowers and bushes. We kept silence long—or a silence only broken by the soft strumming of my guitar. Wilkes was getting impatient; but suddenly a little brown frog bounced out of the water and seated himself on a half-submerged branch of wood, then quickly came a whole congregation out of the muddy water as orderly and noiselessly as Quakers enter meeting. I played soft, now quick, now slow, and still the little ones in brown with their comical little heads and goggle eyes listened attentively. We wanted so much to talk over this wonderful intelligence of our lutarious friends, that I ceased playing; at the sound of our voices a sort of awakening tremor ran in their midst, as we rouse from the enthrallment of some great play, and one by one, with a curious gulping noise of their tiny throats, the audience vanished.

"Well, what do you think of that!" I exclaimed, in triumph.

"It *is* wonderful. I wonder what is the jewel said to be in the toad's head. Perhaps sense, perhaps music. When did you make *this* discovery?"

"I sat here alone all the morning sewing, and singing to myself at times, when suddenly perceiving two funny little things looking at me from the water, I thought of garter-snakes and was about to jump the fence and run, when I recollected our horses stepping in time with our singing. So keeping my place, I sang and watched slyly, till the whole frog family came to the concert. I shall write of this to Dr. Rush," I declared. "With all his great work on the Philosophy of the Human Voice, he does not know its power on frogs. A horse we might more easily understand, having sympathetic feelings, but an ugly, clammy, nasty little frog!"

However, we took frequent delight in amusing the frogs and forgot to trouble our father's old friend with an account of our discoveries. We would not believe the classic tale that a frog's note is a malediction.

A tiny blue-covered book lies near me now, a singular record in verse of the battle of Baltimore and death of Gen. Ross, by Richard Emmons, M.D., 1831. On the flyleaf is written: "From the Author to Mr. Booth." In the back, written hastily in lead penciling, is this list [by Wilkes]:

> *30 for two Steers.*
> *16 for Jessie.*
> *18 for Sukey.*
> _____
> 64
> 25 _____
> 89

One morning as Wilkes was going off on a long ride to Perrymansville to sell some cattle, he wanted something to read on the way, and catching up this little book, he said, "I'll bring it back safely. Don't look so doubtful, I know it was father's."

The black, Henry, helped drive the cattle, and this entry was the amount received for the sale. The writing has not faded in all these thirty [actually, twenty] years. He carefully gave me the book back again, then well scribbled over by children who had had possession of it before we had ever seen it.

In the Dearborn, old Joe drove Wilkes and myself to a far-off country house to inspect some farming utensils that were needed by our workmen. Returning homeward, Wilkes whiled away the time by reciting verses and speeches out of plays: "I come to bury Caesar, not to praise him."

Old Joe broke in with: "De Lord hab mussy on him!"

We dared not laugh at the pious old heart, but after a choking pause Wilkes resumed. "For Brutus was an honorable man."

He was again interrupted. "Dat's a fac, Mass John, he was dat, *jess dat*, was Mass Brutus."

"What's the matter now!" Wilkes said impatiently and in a comical surprise.

"Grandfather always called father *his noble Brutus*, didn't he, Joe?" I asked, giving Wilkes a push to be quiet.

"Jes so, Missy. Ax ole Missus, *she'll* tell you dat an he war too, an hon'able man, if *eber* dar was one," added the old negro emphatically.

We had bought at a country store a packet of candy, and Wilkes quickly produced this. Knowing the negro love of anything sweet, he said, "Have a piece of candy, Joe." It was easy to see this was a device to silence further remarks or criticism, and the old man with chuckles of delight received a stick of peppermint candy. Contrary to our hopes, the kindness and the sweetness combined unloosed the voluble tongue, and oft-repeated tales of "dear old Mass from Ing-land, and Mass Junius Brutus" (our grandfather and our father) came rapidly from the well-stored mind of this respected and at present wearisome old slave.

On an occasion held to be of momentous interest to our Methodist people, everyone had been permitted to attend Camp Meeting. This was a sojourn in some woodland about ten miles distant, and the whole congregation or community remained for a week or ten days, living and sleeping in tents or in camp. The religious exercises were of the most simple and unaffected kind, and these outdoor revivals were often productive of immense and serious good. Our mother went up to Baltimore and left Wilkes, my sister, and self at the farm. Our blacks were to remain ten days and nights at camp.

Very few visitors ever invaded our solitude, but unfortunately, by some contrariety of events, four young ladies were disposed to pay us a visit at this inopportune moment. Hearing the clatter of horses' hoofs and feminine treble afar off among the trees, I rushed to the roof amid the gables, and like Bluebeard's wife's sister gave information to anxious ears below.

"Two ladies on horseback. Two more in sight!"

My sister replied in consternation, "What *shall* we do?"

"Let John know quickly."

"You be ready to entertain them," she said, "we'll have to manage somehow."

Visitors in the country meant all the afternoon and evening entertainment, and we were painfully conscious how low our provisions were. In fact, we had for some time been nearing a state of semi-starvation. Everything had failed. Our mother had amused a fancy of hers by trying what her friends laughed at as ornamental farming, and the result was loss of money, time, and failure of crops. Our cows went obstinately dry sooner than our neighbors' cows; only one generous creature deigned to give us the scantiest supply of milk. This unfortunately was pink milk, and on calling Wilkes' attention to it, saying: "We must have another cow," he remarked, "How great was Shakespeare. He knew everything!"

> *There is an old tale goes-that Herne the*
> *Hunter*
> *Doth all the winter time at still midnight*
> *Walk round about an oak with great ragg'd*
> *horns-*
> *And makes milch-kine yield blood.*
> *Hence we may conclude our Lily-white is*
> *bewitched.*

Our butter was far down in the crock; we had one loaf of wheaten bread left. These scanty supplies passed rapidly through my mind as I made a hasty toilet and descended to open the doors for our guests.

A wretched little five-year-old darky, dressed in a guano-bag frock, came toddling up to the ladies to take one horse at a time. This little black ball of fun and comicality was the only servant at home, being too young to attend camp; and to prevent these self-reliant young ladies from taking their own horses to the stable, I engaged them in a rapid conversation, trying to appear unconcerned and at ease, while my very heart ached in dread, lest that baby slave should get himself trodden upon by the animals or let them run away. Without looking towards the barn I knew that at last the invisible somebody, who was Wilkes in hiding, had received the four horses, that he rubbed them down, and put them up for a rest of six or seven hours.

After an anxious time of forced gaiety and real distress, my sister entered and afforded an opportunity for my escape and the gratification of my curiosity. I found how industriously she had worked. All the best china was set out, and the silver also (which was never to be used), preserves, fresh cresses and radishes, our last bit of meat cut beautifully thin, some delicious fruit decorated with flowers, made the round table beautiful; and on entering the kitchen I beheld our little stock of butter and milk from the dairy, and our last wee loaf ready to be taken to table. John Wilkes was standing at the fire, baking griddle cakes like an experienced cook; he had made the coffee, and I suggested: "Why not have molasses, too! Cakes use up such a quantity of butter."

"Wonderful woman!" he exclaimed, flourishing the batter spoon. "Fly off for it instantly."

When I had brought the molasses in a little glass pitcher, he said demurely: "Now, Asia, pay attention to this. When the cakes are getting low, you must say in a careless nonchalant manner, rising at the same time, just as if we had this kitchen full of slaves but you did not care to trouble them, 'Where is that tiresome darky with the hot cakes? Excuse me a moment, I'll go for them myself.' Then trip out before anyone has a chance to offer to assist—don't you see?—do it gracefully, and I'll have them here for you in a trice."

He came over to the dining-room, saw that everything was in order, and set the covered dish of cakes on the table; then disappeared, as I went in, and begged the visitors to come in to supper.

My sister poured the coffee, and all went well until one lady remarked: "Your brother works very hard on the farm, does he not?"

"Yes," I stammered.

A vision of that scorched face over the kitchen fire was making my mouth twitch, when Rosalie said carelessly: "He'll be in soon, I think."

Glaring at the dish, which was nearly empty, I rose stupidly and muttered something about cakes and darkies. The two younger girls rose immediately and said: "Oh, pray let me go and call him."

"Do let *me* go!"

"Not for the world," I shouted excitedly. "We've got such a fierce dog over in the kitchen!"

Then rushing to the kitchen I snapped out crossly: "Give me the cakes. I'm telling lies enough—we all are—to bring the house down on us."

Wilkes said, handing me the plate covered closely, "A failure; you've forgotten what you had to say. Don't burn yourself."

Not more than fifteen minutes had elapsed before he entered the dining-room in fresh cool toilet, with the easy cheerful manner that characterized him; and saluting the ladies pleasantly, he dropped a kiss on my sister's fore[head] as if he had been absent from home all day and was not in the least hungry.

"I'm afraid these cakes are getting cold, Mr. Booth; let me help you."

"Oh, no, thank you, not for me; I prefer bread."

He ate sparingly of bread and preserves, and took the least drop of milk in his coffee, depriving himself, *we* knew, in order that our little stock might not give out. He proposed the garden, and when there he gathered nosegays for the ladies, which he called *posies*. He surprised them by his town-bred manners, for he knew the language of flowers, and promised to help them write out an alphabetical list of flowers and their significant mottoes. Then seizing an opportune moment he slipped away, saddled and brought up their horses and his own Cola, which he secured near the mounting blocks. The solitary servant was sent toddling up the lane "to set the gates wide open" and then "to hide himself in the barn." The guests had far to go, and Wilkes would accompany them. He assisted the ladies on with their skirts, which in the country were worn over the visiting attire and were removable, and when the moon had well risen, amid many gay farewells, the horses bore away our visitors and our hungry brother.

"Does it ever enter your thoughts," said Rosalie, "that John has worked hard all day and had scarcely any food?"

"Does it occur to your gentle mind," I retorted, "that those friends had ridden far and had country appetites? Our provisions are nearly all gone!"

This was without doubt true, and for three days we three subsisted on the scantiest allowance each, until the arrival of our mother with laden hampers and a supply of money. We could easily have borrowed of a neighbor, or obtained credit at the village store, but although reduced to feel hunger we never entertained that idea of going in debt.

I had seen some of my grandfather's queer little letters to "My dear old comrade and esteemed relative Jack," who was Captain John Brevitt*, which were dated from "Beggarsburg" and "Robinson Crusoe's Island," meaning this same dear old farm, in whose dense confines the good grandfather had, like ourselves, perhaps endured hunger and thirst.

The devices we had resorted to to entertain our guests respectably astonished our mother, who coolly asked, "But why such trouble? Why not have explained the exact state of things?"

This damped the enjoyment we had been having over the recollection of Wilkes' ready adaptability to his several characters of ostler, groom, cook, and host. We had felt, too, a grim

---

*Capt. John Brevitt (1760–1839), an officer in the Second Maryland Regiment during the Revolutionary War.

sort of pleasure in our starvation, while deploring the havoc our guests had made among the edibles; and my stupidity at not being able to "take a part," as Wilkes expressed it, or to tell a little lie with ease, caused them great amusement when it was remembered how readily I had invented one about the ferocious dog in the kitchen.

Mother acknowledged that we had done very well in house-keeping, but would not agree that it was sensible to try "to keep up appearances" to the sacrifice of health and veracity.

Small things define character, the trivialities serve to lighten or to dim a picture otherwise dull or misinterpreted. Such a little thing as a self-imposed abstinence of three days by a boy in strong health, proved a capacity for that after-sacrifice of all of life's goods. And in all such self-abnegation the test of its value is cheerfulness. Men are not at their best so perfect in endurance and resignation as women, and nothing like lack of food so painfully brings out the ugly animal traits of human nature. We could only on reflection admire how merrily our brother gave us the best and greatest share of everything and laughingly strapped in his belt a hole tighter, defying hunger.

At one time Wilkes had ridden many miles to sell some grain at a market station. On his returning homeward he was invited to stop for supper at a friend's house. He was surprised to see that this family, being that of a clergyman, seated themselves at table without saying grace. Pausing a moment to observe what they were about to do, he took his seat with them, blurting out instantly, "Parson Finney, how're oats going?"*

His mind was filled with his recent sale and the marketable prices. Suddenly feeling the silence, he glanced around to find every head bent low over the plates, and the parson's lips moving in inaudible prayer.

"I never felt so contemptible in my life," he said, relating this circumstance. "I tried to apologize, and said that I had been

---

*Rev. William Finney (1789–1873), minister of the Churchville Presbyterian Church, located not far from Tudor Hall.

accustomed to see persons stand to ask the blessing. This made the matter worse, for the sharp old gentleman cut me dead by saying, 'The attitude of prayer is as nothing. The disposition is everything.' He took it of course that I considered *his* attitude as irreverent. I couldn't say more without showing my temper, nor could I refuse to share his meal. Every morsel seemed to stick in my throat, as bad as Macbeth's Amen and I was so confoundedly hungry!"

We spent many hours of the long summer afternoons under the widest-spreading trees, reading aloud from Byron's poems; or seated together in the broad swing under the gum trees and hickories, we would build fantastic temples of fame that were to resound with his name in the days that were coming.

"The Gypsey said I was to have a *grand* life. No matter how short then, so it *be* grand."

He placed almost belief in the old crone's words, and in those days the fortune-tellers held secret but undisputed power, and many well-bred and intelligent people resorted to them. Mother and I often talked of her "vision in the fire," and of her awful dream and linking them with his fortune we let our minds dwell on the possibility that sometime there would come a war, and that Wilkes would be a soldier and die for his country. He too had a vague idea that this fate lurked in the Gypsey's words, for once he said: "The only battle that I'd fight would be against re-election, which means *succession*, and to prevent great privileges falling too easily into foreign hands. None but native-born Americans should fill the chair, and no naturalized citizen should be a candidate; and Washington's refusal of a third term should become as the rock of this Republic."

"Supposing," I said, "that it was possible to nominate a naturalized citizen. Supposing our father had received such an honor!"

"Then," said Wilkes, "I'd have cast *my* vote against him if I'd been of age."

Long arguments followed the slightest divergence into politics, for he loved argument and disputation, and more than once made me late for meals or got me into disgrace through the desire "to clinch an argument." Invariably I fell back upon my sole rock of defense, which was by declaring that no actor should meddle with political affairs, the stage and politics did not go hand in hand, etc., urging him to choose one or the other, for I felt that he had great love for both, and believed him capable of adorning either station. Our childhood was waning fast, even now in its goldenest season, and all too soon he, like the others, must go out and do his work in the world.

Our fields of grain, put in with such hard labor and so eagerly watched, became free pasture for hordes of buzzards and other mischievous birds. He who kills a turkey-buzzard is considered a benefactor, but is worse than a poacher who destroys for the same work of devastation an eatable turkey. Unfortunately, the gun leveled at the illegal trespasser brought down a genuine turkey, and, as misfortune decreed, belonging to our near neighbor who from earliest time had been the most unneighborly. Out of that jealously-guarded field rose up a family cry, as the gobblers and hens that had feasted as plenteously as the buzzards, which the negroes designated as "Warmints," made a hasty departure. We walked briskly to the spot and found to our dismay the dead thing was a large fine turkey. Thinking only of how our mother should have to suffer for this, we got a bag, and like thoughtless children put the dead bird into it and carried it stealthily between us to the woods, by an unused path. When under the trees I let go with a shudder, saying: "Oh, how it makes me tremble! It feels like a human being. Only yesterday we were reading *Eugene Aram*[*], and today we are doing something dreadfully like it."

"Let's take the horrid thing home," Wilkes said, "and then to Wolsey's[†], if mother says so. At least *I* will."

---

[*] A novel (1832) by Bulwer in which a gentleman commits and conceals a murder.

[†] William Woolsey, who died in 1888 at the age of seventy-nine, was one of Harford County's most ambitious and successful farmers.

"No, no," I cried, "let's throw it out of the bag and go home."

Gladly I gathered up the empty bag and we went slowly home, keeping our clumsy secret. I regretted afterward that I had not been wise enough in goodness to have strengthened his honest impulse instead of, Eve-like, tempting him from it.

"But you were not like Adam," I remarked, "in throwing the blame on me."

"I pity Eve, poor little first mother," he said, laughing; "but Adam was a skulk and a sneak, and deserved to have the apple-core stick in his throat."

The next day our near neighbor came and demanded his turkey, and double its price. He had the best of the bargain, and lavished plenty of ill words on us, but although we kept silent, even we children knew how secretly he had removed his neighbor's land-mark until, inch by inch, and year by year, a great piece of the Booth lane had gone to enlarge the Wolsey's meadow.

This transportation of the dead turkey was the grimmest experience in our young days. It had something horrible about it which that fearful poem of Hood's intensified.

> *Ten thousand thousand dreadful eyes*
> *Were looking down in blame.*

All Hallowe'en is kept in country places as a night of wanton and mischievous frolic, when everyone is privileged to pull up his neighbors' cabbages and commit all sorts of harmless depredations. We had some young people from the city stopping with us, and on this fateful night we, the female portion of the family, resorted to the woods in perfect silence, found a hollow stump of a tree that contained the mystic dew with which we bathed our foreheads, and standing apart and silent, waited to greet the expected bridegroom. Those who were fated for a married existence either saw or pretended that they there and then beheld him. After this rite had been solemnly performed, and mysteriously commented upon at home, we prepared to go out on the Hallowe'en raid. We were a large gathering of children and half-grown persons, blacks and whites, and we encountered other parties from the farms and the villages bent on the same errand, and all clothed in silence and the duskiness of night. We carried away gates from farms and set them at a distance, wheeled off carriages and loose wheels from the forge, hid away the blacksmith's tools and the farmers' implements, pulled up cabbages and stacked them where their owners could find them by searching, and leveled the easy snake fences to let the unhoused cattle wander free. It was a cold dark night, with large fiery stars set far up in the black clouds. A perfect starry floor was the heaven that night, and the smell of the earth—which may be the odor of good men's bones rotting, it is so pleasurable and sanctifying—the aroma of the pines, and the rapturous sense of a solemn silence, made us feel happy enough to sing "Te Deum Laudamus." But the Hallowe'en robbers must go without a sound.

Arrived by a circuitous road at one side of our grounds, we beheld at our own gate our poor old white horse George, standing tied by his halter with a large cabbage fastened to his neck. We had to sit, or fall down with silent laughter that we tried desperately to stifle, but we opened the gate and turned him on his own domain, leaving the cabbage at his throat. In another place, we found our fences laid low, and being very fatigued, and these little darkies falling about in weariness, we turned homeward. Going down an incline, Wilkes, seeing the rest safely over the marsh to the road, stopped me on a hillock, saying something about the stars. We paused a moment, when a loud report startled us and a shower of shot rattled down upon us. He threw me flat on my face and laid upon me, nearly crushing me by the quickness. Then followed shower after shower, and loud reports which went reverberating in endless echoes. After this he sprang up, fiercely shaking his fist towards the forgotten little hut in the hollow, which was the home of the negro, Stephen Hooper*, shouting out: "I'll

---

*A free farmer about forty years old with an extensive family of children who lived in the immediate neighborhood.

remember you for this, Stephen Hooper!"

No black was allowed the use of firearms, and this man had had no provocation even, but he had seen our figures on the rise above the road and had dared to use his gun. Being a black man and so near our own place, we had left him undisturbed and were, at this time of returning home, too tired to attempt any more robberies. Wilkes' soft felt hat was riddled by shot, and his indignation was great, but he picked up a howling little black, who was frightened, and set him across his shoulders to carry him home.

"Me's shooted, Mars' Johnnie. Me's shooted!"

"You're not touched, you little black ape! Curl up on Johnnie's shoulder, and go to sleep."

And the true darky, ever ready for sleep, seemed instantly to obey, for the woolly pate fell on the strong head of Wilkes, and in a short time he said in a low voice as if not to awaken him: "How that monkey snores up there!"

When the season came again to hire labor (some of Stephen's family, who by their mother were half-bloods and *not* slaves, had been frequently at work for us), I asked Wilkes to induce mother to leave out these Hoopers. "Remember Hallowe'en," I said.

"Oh, no," Wilkes said relentingly, "revenge is so mean. Against a darky too! Somehow, I've forgiven Stephen."

"I have not," I said stoutly, "nor shall I forget that a black man dared to fire on us even with shot." We knew how easy it would have been to put Stephen Hooper in a jail, and knew he nursed a smiling hatred for us because he knew that he had done us an injury and we had spared him. Wilkes said, looking seriously up from a fence rail he was repairing, holding the hammer in one hand and the nail in the fingers of the other, "Do you know that I believe you have a tinge of Jewish blood. You always cry revenge, and I notice that it strains your heart to forgive."

I laughed at the words then, but time with its cruel wrongs has forced me to acknowledge that it does "strain my heart to forgive."

Wilkes added thoughtfully, "Much of the evil of us boys and girls, some of the good as well, must have been engendered by power of those furious plays our father enacts. The Shylock, and Pescara, mad-seeming Hamlet, and love-sick Romeo, et cetera, et cetera," he added with quick emphasis. And with his face red with blushes he hammered at the fence rail.

I said nothing, but thought, without shame, of his words. In these years I ponder them and think how modest he was always in speech and action.

A man had the farm on shares, for our mother had tried various ways of making what she called "a living out of this useless land" and what Wilkes called "trying to starve respectably by torturing the barren earth." Great hopes were entertained that this fresh attempt might be rewarded with success. The man was to work our horses, which he did mercifully enough at first, but he was ambitious of "turning out the best crops in Harford." He nearly ruined my mother by purchases of guano, and then he worked men, himself, and our beasts until her patience was exhausted. It was pitiable to see our dumb creatures droop in the fields, too tired to drag themselves homeward. Mother at last remonstrated, when he excitedly told her to "mind her own business." She objected to let her horses go to the fields unless the men were allowed to return at sundown, and the horses be then housed. The man became very insolent and called her and us vile names, which my mother related to Wilkes when he returned home in the evening. He was accompanied by a friend who was a practicing lawyer. This gentleman told him "to come down to the lodge and demand an apology from the man, and then arrange about the hours of work for men and beasts."

"Apologize!" Wilkes said; "He's not the sort of man to do that. I'll get a stick ready."

He cut for himself a stout stick, and the two walked down to the lodge. The friend of Wilkes called out the farmer, and Wilkes demanded an apology being made to the ladies.

"First find your *ladies*," the farmer insolently retorted.

"Will you go up to my house this moment with me, and apologize to my mother and sisters for the abusive names you have called them?"

"Do *you* think I am going to lose my share of these crops just to save a lot of lazy dumb beasts and thickskulled niggers from being *tired*? Apologize! That won't *I*!"

"Then," said Wilkes, "I'll whip you like the scoundrel that you are." And he let the stick fall heavily on the head and shoulders of the man who yelled out noisily that "he was killed and murdered."

Wilkes' friend caught his hand when he considered that the farmer had had a good thrashing, and the three walked up to their respective homes. The farmer, however, soon emerged from the door with his head bound up and took his way to that near neighbor's whose turkey we had slaughtered and hidden in the woods. Their advice to him was, "to have us all bound over to keep the peace," for which purpose they lent the farmer their cart and horse to go next day to Bel Air, as he assured us, "to swear his life against us."

Our friend managed to have the court brought out to us, to save us the annoyance of going in procession to the magistrate at Bel Air. Accordingly this gentleman arrived in company with the magistrate and a clerk. We were brought into the room, not a very belligerent looking company. My mother in her widow's weeds, my gentle invalid sister, Wilkes, very handsome, and I, very cross, a half score of darkies evincing every attitude of idiocy and terror, and the little blacks of tender age. The least of these, naked but for the half guano sack tied about waist and thighs (for it is as difficult to keep clothing on these children of nature as to keep the web-footed tribe from water), was asked his name.

"D'no."

On being pressed to think of his name, he uttered, with a loud yell of laughter, "*Pink.*"

And after much amusement this farcical court dissolved, and we felt ourselves bound over to keep the peace.

The darky capability of turning everything ludicrous or otherwise into a hymn was noticed by us frequently. We were not much surprised then at hearing the young ones improvise this event. Shouting in chorus and clapping their hands they uttered,

We's bound over to keep the peace,
To keep the peace, to keep the peace,
We's all bound over to keep the peace,
Glory halleluyah!

The farmer, who fortunately was only scratched, but well bruised on the shoulders and pained in conscience, agreed to forbear in his maltreatment of our black men and horses and require no more of them than they could reasonably do between sun-up and sunset.

The last winter we passed on the farm was one of intense cold, and we endured great privation. Our stock died off. We never killed as our neighbors did, and it was only on rare occasions that we could effect a purchase of fresh meat. We were literally snowed in and every kind of provision was failing. We regarded the creatures and feathered tribe about our dwellings as silent members of the family, which even if we had slaughtered, we could not partake of. Mother said, "This comes of you children naming and making pets of every bird and beast."

We had let loose a cage of five partridges, because they looked so pretty, but mother herself said "they were too beautiful to destroy." The sheer necessity of the case led us to set traps beyond our own precincts, quite in the pine woods, which belonged to no one and where all sorts of wild things strayed at large. All in a night, as it were, the snow had fallen and lay thick and deep everywhere. The drifts were alarming to behold, but on the second day we thought of the traps, and dared to go through the drift to the opposite side of the main road. Wilkes found the fence by means of his long pole, and, mounting the

top rail, successfully leaped the highest drift, falling in a pile
up to his waist.

"Now, leap like that," he said to me, "and you're all right."
I leaped short of it and sank up to my throat.

He laughed wildly. "Where are you gone!" But at the same
time he worked with dexterous haste to level the drift, for it
covered me up like a sea of feathers. I was at length released,
and he expended the remainder of his strength in laughter,
while I shivered and scolded by turns.

After a series of difficulties we reached the traps to find a
wild-eyed opossum and another ugly starving creature, both
past wailing, evidently awaiting their doom of death in silent
heroism. We made this excursion to fetch home something for
ourselves to eat, something not killed upon our own place, but
instead we set at liberty animals more hungry than ourselves.
All at once Wilkes looked at me and exclaimed, "That's smart!
We've thrown away two or three meals, and these creatures
had quite made up their minds to die."

How quickly they had changed their unspoken minds we
were allowed to judge by the fleetness with which they em-
braced their liberty.

The road as far as we could discern was an unspotted bed of
snow, soft, feathery and deep, treacherously deep, with drifts
piled high over the gulches on either side, making certain
graves for the unwary traveler; but none ever put foot upon
the roads until the heavy broad-wheeled wagons began to leave
their traces on the solid earth.

Meanwhile we came near to sickness through want of nour-
ishing food. Joyously now Wilkes set off to a distant farm to
purchase a milch cow. He was belated and nearly frozen to
death, was taken into the neighbor's house speechless and
half asleep, then rubbed and whipped awake, and restored
by brandy. He had intended to drive the cow home in the
night, but while we sat waiting through the dismal hours for
his return, he was carefully tucked away in a warm bed. Late in
the following day he arrived home, driving an important black

cow before him; which, on account of her grand appearance and the name of her previous owner, Parker Lea, we called at once "Lady Parker." We soon had draughts of warm good milk, and no butter ever was so eagerly watched as that which came of the first churning. We three, Wilkes, my sister and self, took turns at the dasher, and were so fearful of letting the "churning go back," as the country folk say, but we could not easily forget that to enjoy these luxuries we had risked our boy's life.

The Know-Nothing meetings were a so-called "debating society," where the question of putting a limit to white labor was contested. This, it was feared, would eventually supersede that of the blacks, and great privileges were falling too easily into the hands of the unnaturalized Irish immigrants. The Know-Nothing meetings were exciting to riots and contention, the women everywhere taking sides in the momentous question. Near us there was to be held a great mass meeting, and Henry Winter Davis[*], an eminent orator, was announced to address the people. The country was enthusiastic in his praise, and everyone eager to attend the meeting.

That was oratory worth hearing! Not humorous and rife with similitude and quotations, but coming direct from an impassioned heart and a cultivated mind; beautiful thoughts were clothed in choice words, and every sentence, delivered in his clear ringing voice, appealed to the hearts and intellects of his auditors. He could be sarcastic and persuasive too, and although this was only a stump oration it was chaste and elegant.

Wilkes was one of the stewards and was decorated with a badge of colors. He was dispatched to bring a banner from Bel Air, which had been forgotten; it was to help in draping the platform. As he passed down the crowded road on his Cola the edge of the bank gave way under his horse's feet and brought him to the ground. He leaped off, hoisted the colt, and, by aid

---

[*]Henry Winter Davis (1817–1865), elected to the House of Representatives on the American Party ticket by this 1854 campaign.

of the flag-staff, without touching the stirrup, sprang lightly into the saddle and dashed off again, only looking back at us with a reassuring smile. Arriving at the place of meeting, we beheld him the center of a group of ladies, who were brushing his coat and otherwise expressing sympathy with the standard bearer.

The dress of that day was considered fashionable when contrasting in colors. Wilkes wore a dark claret cloth coat with velvet lapels, a pale buff waistcoat and dove-colored trousers lightly strapped down under the boot; a broad guayaquil straw hat with a broad black ribbon band completed a costume pronounced elegant. He was always well dressed, and on this particular occasion looked remarkably handsome.

Wilkes went for a brief visit to Baltimore, and on the day of his return I was under the low trees outside our grounds pulling mandrakes, gathering may-apples and dew-berries. Six little darkies, seven dogs, and a couple of cats who always followed the dogs, were my company. Our baskets were partly filled, and the clatter of hoofs sounding clear, I looked out from the bushes to see Wilkes returning on Cola. He came up rapidly then and dismounted, while the dogs yelped and the cats rubbed against his legs, and the piping querulous voices of the darkies called out in the uproar, "How do, Mars' Johnnie."

He had a greeting for all and threw a packet of candies from his saddle-case far beyond where we stood, saying, "After it, Nigs! Don't let the dogs get it!"

The never-forgotten bag of candies was longingly looked for by the blacks, young and old, whenever "Mars' Johnnie" came from town or village.

Turning to me, he said, "Well, Mother Bunch*, guess what I've done!" Then answering my silence, he said, "I've made my first appearance on any stage, for this night only, and in big capitals."

---

*A Mother-Goose figure, familiar from fairy tales.

He had acted "Richmond" at the St. Charles' Theatre, Baltimore*. His face shone with enthusiasm, and by the exultant tone of his voice it was plain that he had passed the test night. He had made his venture in life and would soon follow on the road he had broken. Mother was not so pleased as we to hear of this adventure; she thought it premature, and that he had been influenced by others who wished to gain notoriety and money by the use of his name.

We sat in the old swing-seat late that night, indulging romantic fancies. "He could never hope to be as great as father, he never wanted to try to rival Edwin, but he wanted to be loved of the Southern people above all things. He would work to make himself essentially a Southern actor."

He applied himself studiously to Shakespeare, and I was made to hear parts over and over again for my slow student. He would not allow a word or syllable to go wrong, and "Julius Caesar," that test part for the theatrical scholar, was so constantly repeated that even the little darkies, whose privilege was to sit and loll about in the corners of whatever rooms we occupied, were caught repeating after him.

"Hark to that thick-skulled darky! She has sharper wits than I," Wilkes lamented when vainly trying to give a speech correctly.

"Richard the Third" was far easier to retain, and "Shylock," but he said doubtingly, "I can never be a nimble skip-about like Romeo; I am too square and solid."

Those days of study were prosy days, and our struggles with the ever-open manuscript, which we called "The Memoir of Booth the Elder," had somewhat interfered with the lightheartedness, the poetry and music, and long aimless rambles on foot and horseback. We were very studious. The seriousness of life had come, the last happy days of childhood were recollections only. Each of us children, who had grown earnest,

---

*Asia should have identified this premature debut in the play "Richard III" as taking place at the Charles Street Theatre, August 14, 1855.

loving, and gentle with human tenderness for all living and inanimate things, went out from the solemn old woods for ever.

The weird tales of Hawthorne, the heart-songs of Thomas Hood, the exquisite rhythmic religious poems of Tom Moore, the never-old unrhyming poesy of Shakespeare, softened each wild fancy and cheered each somber mood, as well in the busy world to which we were removed as they had soothed, calmed, or excited us in the solitudes.

In loneliness and isolation of spirit or of body, the poet is best beloved because best understood. Quotations familiarize and endear him to us, the verses that suit our state or feeling link us mysteriously to his joy or pain, and we become as part of him when we beautify our dull prose with gems of his broken verse. Those whom solitude has forced to learn and love this unsung music must retain its meaning and its sweetness as consolation till the end.

In the summer of 1857 he joined the company at the Arch St. Theatre, Philadelphia, playing a very small character in "The Belle's Stratagem."

Wilkes appeared in Baltimore in connection with his brother Edwin, acting "Richmond" to Edwin's "Richard."* A Quakeress who had never entered a theater before was present at this performance. Her description of Wilkes was, "He made me feel what a tyrant Richard had been. I seemed actually to be living at that time instead of in this quiet century. As for his appearance—well, he looked like a new blown rose with the morning dew upon it."

The most interesting part of this life cannot be afforded at the present writing, as all information contained in criticisms, letters, playbills and theatrical records, has been lost in the general destruction of papers and effects belonging to Wilkes Booth. All written or printed material found in our possession, everything that bore his name was given up, even the little

---

*This performance was given at the Holliday Street Theatre, Baltimore, on August 27, 1858.

picture of himself, hung over my babies' beds in the nursery. He had placed it there himself saying, "Remember me, babies, in your prayers." Not a vestige remains of aught that belonged to him; his books of music were stolen, seized, or savagely destroyed. The old diaries from which I transcribe had before that time been in the keeping of a friend, but these furnish no further record of his brief stage life than the few occasions noted here.

In 1859 Wilkes came from Richmond, where he was fulfilling an engagement, to be present at my wedding. He returned to that city immediately after the wedding; he was not pleased at my marriage, and the strange words he whispered to me were, "Always bear in mind that you are a professional stepping-stone. Our father's name is a power—theatrical—in the land. It is dower enough for any struggling actor."

He was become very popular in the South, yet he sadly felt the need of a less enthusiastic school. They loved him "for his father's sake," and he yearned for criticism, no matter how severe, if just. He had no master to form his style upon. His admiration of [Edwin] Forrest was enthusiastically expressed.* Wilkes had a great and sincere affection for John McCullough as a man, and unbounded admiration for him as an actor. He said that "McCullough ought to become in the future Forrest's son and heir—I mean theatrically—for he is the only one worthy of wearing the old Roman's sandals." James Murdock was his ideal of grace and perfect elocution, E. L. Davenport he admired for finish and correctness; but he said, "These are not as father was to Edwin. If *I* shine at all, it must be in the rough. Consider how much Edwin has to contend with, being called an imitator of father, frequently by those who do not even know how to compare the two. He will always have to fight against the spiteful judgment of his detractors, based upon his long association with his father. Whatever talent *you*

---

*Forrest (1806–1872), Murdoch (1811–1893), McCullough (1832–1885), and Davenport (1815–1877) were leading tragedians during the Civil War period.

may possess will be nature's own legacy. Only be persevering through all things."

Wilkes had acted a short engagement at the Broadway Theatre, New York, in March, 1862. It was the first wearing away of family affection. Although he by no means ever sought to place himself in opposition to Edwin, he felt it rather premature that Edwin should mark off for himself the North and the East, and leave the South where he no longer cared to go himself, to Wilkes. He felt that he had not had a chance in New York, and his Southern friends were fervid in their desire to make him prove himself in the cities of the North and East. He was having a wrong tuition in the ardent South, where even his errors were extolled and his successes magnified. The people loved him; he had never known privation or want, was never out of an engagement, while Edwin had had the rough schooling of poverty, hardship in far distant cities, struggles in his professional experience, fiercer struggles with himself. He had gone through the drudgery of his art through the fire of temptation, and he overcame and was victorious.

Before my third child was born, Wilkes wished to have the expected boy called John Wilkes. At a raffle in the South he won a prize, and on being called up the crowded room to receive it, a complete suit of infant's clothing was carefully deposited in his arms amid great laughter and pleasantry.

"I was dreadfully shame-faced," he wrote, "but all at once, like a blessing, I recollected my expected nephew and was able to reply confidently, 'These are most acceptable, ladies. I am in hourly expectation of the safe arrival of a little nephew or niece.' Quick as thought then the health and safety of mother and babe were wished, and I walked down the long room carrying my babyclothes which shall be sent you express. P.S. Asia, I thank you for the coming child."

This child, a girl, was named Adrienne after her uncle, Joseph Adrien Booth, who had received the name of Adrien on account of J. B. Booth junior acting "Adrien de Mauprat" so well. Wilkes was, as he said, willing to wait for the boy to bear *his* name.

He acted continuously, traveled much, and accumulated a great deal of money. He bought land and speculated in oil wells. Success attended all his undertakings. He left Richmond and unsought enrolled himself as one of the party going to search for and capture John Brown. He was exposed to dangers and hardships. He was a scout, and I have been shown a picture of himself and others in their scout and sentinel dresses. He was a witness of the death of old John Brown. He acknowledged him a hero when he saw him die, and felt a throb of anguish as he beheld the old eyes straining their anxious sight for the multitude he vainly had thought would rise to rescue him.

"He was a brave old man; his heart must have broken when he felt himself deserted." Uttering these words sadly, he gave me the spear of old Brown, with "Major Washington to J. Wilkes Booth" written in large ink letters on the handle.[*]

This fearful war scattered dissension in families, as well as disunion abroad. Sons of the same mother fought by sea and by land against each other. So intermingled by marriage and by love were the North and South, that scarcely a family felt unreservedly for either side.

Wilkes worked indefatigably; he made great sums of money, so did other theatrical men. It was the harvest time for theaters, the years of that disastrous war, but Wilkes hoarded, saved, grew miserly at last. He expressed himself bitterly against the North, but he acted North and traveled among Northerners indiscriminately.

Edwin Booth lived with his mother in New York, and, although it was Edwin's house, it became the stopping place of the brothers from time to time. Edwin would not listen to Wilkes' hot denunciation of the Northern policy, and nothing grated this fierce Southern partisan so sorely as beholding the easy enlistment of Irishmen who were wild to free the "nagur" before they had even looked upon a black face.

---

[*]Major Lewis Washington (1812–1871), a hostage of John Brown during the abolitionist's raid at Harpers Ferry in 1859. Booth was present for Brown's execution, but not his capture.

"It is the unwisest move this country has yet made," he would exclaim. "The suave pressing of hordes of ignorant foreigners, buying up citizens before they land, to swell their armies. It is a thing Americans will blush to remember one day when Patrick coolly tells them that *he won their battles for them, that he fought and bled and freed the nagur.* The time will come, whether conquered or conqueror, when the braggart North will groan at not being able to swear they fought the South man for man. If the North conquer us it will be by numbers only, not by native grit, not pluck, and not by devotion."

"*If the North conquers us*—we are of the North," I said.

"Not I, not I!" he said excitedly. "So help me holy God! my soul, life, and possessions are for the South."

"Why not go fight for her, then? Every Marylander worthy the name is fighting her battles."

He sat silent long, and with his thin face hard-set; then uttered slowly after I had bitterly repented my quick speech, "I have only an arm to give; my brains are worth twenty men, my money worth a hundred. I have free pass everywhere. My profession, my name, is my passport. My knowledge of drugs is valuable, my beloved precious money—oh, never beloved till now!—is the means, one of the means, by which I serve the South."

I questioned him closely on his ease in going everywhere among Northern armies, asked what he was doing in Texas, Kansas, etc.

"I believe you have Grant's pass," I ventured.

"Just so," he answered to my consternation. "U.S.—United States as he wants to be called, but they swear South that it is not his name—has given me freedom of range without knowing what a good turn he has done the South. Not that the South cares a bad cent about *me*, mind—a mere peregrinating play-actor," he added in explanation.

He sat smiling grimly in self-communion, and presently I said in a low voice, "A man came here the other day for *Doctor* Booth. What does that mean? I fancied it was some one who had known Joseph as medical student at Philadelphia, or with Dr. [Columbus Da Vega] at the South, but. . . ."

"All right," he said lightly, "I am he, if to be a doctor means a dealer in quinine."

"The drug that the North says is more in requisition than food for the Southerners?"

"Yes." The real genuine quinine was a most expensive drug; he rejoiced that he had not only plenty of money to buy it, but knew people who supplied him with the perfect article, there was so much paltry stuff called by the name employed in northern hospitals. Wilkes was an expert in this matter.

"You send it! How?"

"Horse-collars and so forth," he laughed.

"You run the blockade?"

"Yes."

"You are doing as F.B. and his young wife of Harford did when they smuggled arms South in wagon loads of grain?"

He laughed and said, "Think of those two little birds of fashion, disguised as rough country people and carrying out such a plot as that!"

In vain I talked of danger. The circumstances and penalties of war were known to me only in histories. I could not believe him safe or beyond danger at any time, knowing his Southern principles, but I knew he had wisdom and was not a man to chatter his affairs to every listener. Rather that faculty for listening to others was brought to serve his purpose now; he led on others to talk and disclose their minds, while he held silence and acquired much knowledge that served against them. I knew now that my hero was a spy, a blockade-runner, a rebel! I set the terrible words before my eyes, and knew that each one meant death. I knew that he was today what he had been from childhood, an ardent lover of the South and her policy, an upholder of Southern principles. In spite of my bitter taunt, I knew that if he had twenty lives they would be sacrificed freely for that cause. He was a man so single in his devotion, so unswerving in his principles, that he would yield everything for the cause he espoused. *Ever faithful* was oftentimes the only ending of his boyish letters from Catonsville. The words might serve as his epitaph, for he was, in love, friendship, and in principle, ever faithful.

I found myself trying, despite the school training on the subject, to think with less detestation of those two despicable characters in history, Major André and Benedict Arnold.

He was once stopping at Edwin's New York house, and, suffering from a diseased arm [an erisyphilis attack, in August, 1864], he fainted from the acute pain, and Junius carried him and laid him upon his bed. As he lay there in his shirt-sleeves so pale and death-like, we all felt how wondrously beautiful he was. It was a picture that took hold deeply of our hearts, for soon he was to lie dead among his foes, and not one of us should gaze upon his face. As we saw it then, pallid and death-like on his bed, we were to ponder it all our lives.

Wilkes had laughed grimly at the thought of having carried Adam Badeau* to and from Edwin's house.

"Imagine me," he said, "helping that wounded soldier with my rebel sinews! If it were not for mother I would not enter Edwin's house, but she will leave there if we cannot be welcomed, and I do not want her to be unhappy for me. As for Clarke," he added, "we are as the Antipodes, and I would never darken his door, but for you."

There were some stormy words between the two brothers Edwin and Wilkes, the first, and, I believe, the last unkind ones that ever passed between them.

Wilkes came to my house in Philadelphia, and a doctor—strangely enough a Quaker doctor who was sent in the place of our family physician—lanced a great carbuncle on his neck. The things required were set on the table, and in removing a lampshade the hose of the gas caught in the flame and was burning quickly when Wilkes crushed it in his hands and

---

*Adam Badeau (1831–1895), a close friend of Edwin's who was then serving as a staff officer for General U. S. Grant.

bound it up hurriedly with a bit of dress braid. His neck was lanced, and he suffered much. His system was overworked and needed rest, and when I took his burned hands in mine, I wondered to find how rugged and hard the palms were. He confessed to "nights of rowing," furthermore "to wearing several suits of underclothes." The boots that reached to his thighs had pistol-holsters in them. The shabby, worn hat and coat were not evidence of recklessness but of care for others, self-denial, to result in self-immolation.

Junius Booth dearly loved this one of his brothers; he admired his athletic beauty, and loved him for his nature, his disposition and that irresistible fascination which few men could resist. There were qualities in Wilkes which seemed to stamp him for a leader among men, but this idea lost hold in Junius' mind, when he stood one night with him in the streets of Washington, and beheld the tears run from his eyes as he turned his face towards Richmond, saying brokenly, "Virginia—Virginia."

It was like a wail from the heart of the Roman father over his slaughtered child. This idealized city of his love had deeper hold upon his heart than any feminine beauty; but this very weakness of tears was proof of the depth of his strength.

He had in these troublesome days of that long war mingled with all sorts of people, as he rushed from state to state pursuing his profession. He was a welcome guest in the highest circles of society and ingratiated himself with ladies of distinction. From them he gathered much to serve his purpose, observed "how women rule the nation," he said, and even while on desperate work intent he "undesignedly fell in love with a senator's daughter." The attachment resulted in a secret and conditional engagement.

He was heard from in Kansas, Canada, New Orleans. His restless, fiery life seemed a charmed one and he was powerful to throw off fatigue and pain, to crush out lassitude and disinclination. He was known everywhere by his large loosely-hanging light overcoat, with its deep sleeves and cape, and his low soft hat. His was not a face or figure to go unremarked. He was easily recognizable, but as he had said, "his name and his profession were his passport."

He gave the greater part of a day to the torturing composition of a valentine acrostic to send to the lady of his love. Junius tried to be serious over his poetic agonies, but they recalled the labors of the boy at school, and now it seemed as difficult to invent as it had been to remember. Unheeding the amusement he caused, he persevered, even through the night, and the next morning he triumphantly read out his easy flowing verses; the result of his lucubration was a success. The following passage from a letter by Junius Booth after he and Wilkes had returned to New York alludes to this valentine. The date, the Tuesday before February 14th, 1865.

> *John (Wilkes) sat up all Monday night to put Miss H's Valentine in the mail, and slept on the sofa so as to be up early; kept me up last night till 3 ½ A.M. to wait while he wrote her a long letter—kept me awake by every now and then using me as a Dictionary. He says he shall remain here till Wednesday. The dumb and deaf poetess, Miss R—, you and I were speaking about, is here; John is acquainted with her and is practising his fingers to talk with her.* * *Since his Acrostic he is resolved to cultivate the muse.*

One day I asked casually after the fate of Michael O'Laughlin†, who was in Beauregard's army. Wilkes looked up with a start that drove the color from his face.

"Michael!" he said. "Why, what possessed you to—to ask about *him*? He's home, on leave," he added more calmly.

---

*Lucy Hale (1842–1915), daughter of Senator John P. Hale and the last romantic interest of Booth's life. Laura Redden Searing (1840–1923), poet and Civil War correspondent.

†Michael O'Laughlen (1840–1867), childhood friend of Booth's and Confederate soldier who entered his abduction plot against Lincoln.

"Home on leave in war time!" I said. "Not in the hospital then?"

"No," Wilkes rejoined. "Forget his name, don't talk of him!"

He said this sadly, not as if Michael was dead though, and not as if they had quarreled. This early friend was one of those convicted of the Conspiracy, the one who died at the Dry Tortugas.

In November, 1864, the play of "Julius Caesar" was produced at the Winter Garden Theatre, New York. The three brothers assumed the characters of Brutus, Cassius, and Marc Antony. Edwin was nervous; he admired Wilkes and thought that he never beheld a being so perfectly handsome. I think he trembled a little for his own laurels. In the densely packed theater I heard from my standing-place many comments on the merits of the brothers. One voice said delightedly, *"Our Wilkes* looks like a young god."

I turned to see a Southerner with eyes intently watching the play.

This performance and that engagement of one week's duration in 1862 were the only occasions of Wilkes Booth appearing in New York. He enacted "Pescara" for the benefit of John McCullough at Washington, [on March 18, 1865] and that was his last appearance upon the stage.

Fierce scenes of terror and bloodshed, of riots and raids, were daily enacted at this wild time of the war. Wilkes came frequently to me at Philadelphia, or rather, to my husband's house. I saw and heard much that distressed and surprised me, but my husband was a careless steward of his own affairs, and never gave a thought to the direction or management of his own household. Wilkes knew that he could come and go at our house unquestioned and unobserved. He often slept in his clothes on the couch downstairs, having on his long riding boots. Strange men called at late hours, some whose voices I knew, but who would not answer to their names; and others who were perfectly strange to me. They never came farther than the inner sill, and spoke in whispers.

One night, Wilkes was more than usually excited; he looked haggard and worn. I heard him murmur, "Oh, God, grant me to see the end!"

I said, "Do not go South again, my poor brother, do not go."

"Why, where *should* I go then?" he said, opening his eyes wide in astonishment, as if the South held his heartstrings. Then he sang low and distinctly a wild parody, each verse ending with a rhyme to a year, then, "In 1865 when Lincoln shall be king."

I said, "Oh, not that. That will *never* come to pass!"

"No, by God's mercy," he said, springing to his feet.

"Never *that!*" Then he whispered fiercely, "That Sectional Candidate should never have been President, the votes were *doubled* to seat him.* He was smuggled through Maryland to the White House. Maryland is true to the core—every mother's son. Look at the cannon on the heights of Baltimore. It needed just that to keep her quiet. This man's appearance, his pedigree, his coarse low jokes and anecdotes, his vulgar similes, and his policy are a disgrace to the seat he holds. Other brains rule the country. *He* is made the tool of the North, to crush out, or try to crush out slavery, by robbery, rapine, slaughter and bought armies. He is walking in the footprints of old John Brown, but no more fit to stand with that rugged old hero—Great God! No. John Brown was a man inspired, the grandest character of this century! *He* is Bonaparte in one great move, that is, by overturning this blind Republic and making himself a king. This man's re-election which will follow his success, I tell you, will be a reign! The subjects, bastard subjects, of other countries, apostates, are eager to overturn this government. You'll see, you'll see that *re-election* means *succession*. His kin and friends are in every place of office already. Trust the songs of the people. They are the bards, the troubadors. Who make these songs if not the people!

---

*Meaning unclear. There were no irregularities in the count of the 1860 electoral vote.

'Vox populi' forever! These false-hearted, unloyal foreigners it is, who would glory in the downfall of the Republic—and that by a half-breed too, a man springing from the ashes of old Assanothime Brown*, a false president yearning for kingly succession as hotly as ever did Ariston."†

A desperate turn towards the evil had come! I had listened so patiently to these wild tirades, which were the very fever of his distracted brain and tortured heart, that I was powerless to check or soothe. Every person was fierce in condemnation of the South. There was never a relenting word or pity for their terrible loss; only fierce, savage, diabolical joy over every list of defeat and slaughter. The most vindictive and venomous tongues were those of women—not American born women. The North had a serpent tongue and a cruel red hand uppermost.

He had sat late with me on one of these nights—the last—and said to me, "Let me show you the cipher."‡

When I understood what he meant, I said, "No, I shall not consent to any knowledge of that kind."

But he added, "I might possibly need to communicate with you about my money affairs, and there is no need to let everyone know what I am worth."

I resisted, and then he said, taking a large packet from his breast, "Lock this in your safe for me. I may come back for it, but if anything should happen to me open the packet *alone* and send the letters as directed, and the money and papers give to their owners."

It was not unusual to speak thus of possible accidents, for in these reckless times the travel was rough and incessant, and a traveling actor's life is one of exposure to danger. I promised

---

*So called from his antislavery activities near Osawatomie, Kansas Territory, in 1855.

†Greek philosopher (d. 87 B.C.) whose ambition led to his becoming tyrant of Athens.

‡A "court cipher" or code later found by authorities among Booth's possessions.

to lock up the packet. He kissed me many times good-by, and I sat where he had left me looking at the long envelope in my lap, with the one word "Asia" written on it. In a few moments he returned, and said, "Let me *see* you lock up the packet."

Together we unfastened the heavy door, then unbarred the inner iron one, then entered the room of stone and iron, and I stooped and placed the packet in the iron safe. We made all secure, and I hid the last key away. As I sat on the sofa, he came and knelt down at my feet, and laid his head in my lap. After a little time, during which I smoothed his black hair carelessly, he said, looking in my face, "When will your child be born, my girl?"

"In five months, I think, or less."

"I hope you will keep well and get stronger, dear."

Then as we rose together, he kissed me very tenderly and said, "God bless you, sister mine. Take care of yourself, and try to be happy."

"Oh, my boy," I said, with all the anxiety of my heart, "I shall never be happy till I see your face again."

There is no more to add. The rest is horror, fitter for a diary than for these pages. In time the blow fell on us, a loving, united and devoted family. And in time an enraged and furious Government did us much bitter wrong, and some justice. The packet I opened alone and destroyed an envelope with a man's name written upon it. (It is a name since numbered with the dead.) The ashes of this paper I blew about the room for safety, and the letter, with another envelope addressed S. K. Chester[*], I handed to my husband and the others who stood near. The packet contained, besides this, bonds or coupons for his mother, a transfer of an oil well to Junius Booth, another for his sister Rosalie. His Boston land was afterwards given by his mother to her son Joseph, and I retained the envelope marked "Asia." This was afterwards taken from me.

---

[*]Chester (1836–1921), actor, childhood friend of Booth who attempted to lure him into the abduction plot.

Above all his kind love to me, I thanked him most that he left me nothing. Had he done so, it would have put a whip in my foe's hand, to torture my remaining life. Mr. J. S. Clarke thoughtlessly gave that enclosed letter alluding to a kidnapping scheme to Mr. Stockton, his personal friend and the reporter of a daily paper, and, as every shred of news was voraciously accepted, the letter was published, and arrests followed in quick succession.

It was like the days of the Bastille in France. Arrests were made suddenly and in dead of night. No reason or warning given, only let anyone breathe a doubt of the most innocent person and arrest followed swift, and that incarceration meant to wait the law's leisure, innocent or guilty. Detectives, women and men, decoys, and all that vile rabble of human bloodhounds infested the city.

Junius Booth, who was in Cincinnati acting, came to our house. He was arrested, but the officer politely put the handcuffs in his own pocket and allowed the prisoner to walk unmanacled at two o'clock in the morning. A few nights later J. S. Clarke was arrested, and both were placed in the Old Capitol Prison at Washington. Joseph Booth, who had arrived after three and a half years' trip to Australia, was arrested before landing and placed in jail in New York. Edwin Booth was surrounded by influential friends, but with an outer guard of spies to note his movements.

This unfortunate publication, so useless now when the scheme had failed—and it led to no fresh discoveries—brought a host of miseries, for it not only served for food to newsmongers and enemies, but it directed a free band of male and female detectives to our house. The newspapers called on "servants to be spies upon their employers in the cause of the Government." My house, which was an extensive (*mysteriously built*, it was now called) old mansion, was searched; then, without warning, surprised by a full body of police, surrounded, and searched again. We were under hourly surveillance from outside, and I, left alone, received the visit of a young official who had a carriage and pair at the door to conduct me to Washington. To this young man of twenty-one years perhaps, I was obliged to state my condition of health, and he advised me to procure a certificate to the effect that I was unable to travel. The old doctor who had brought me through much illness could with difficulty be induced to come to my house, but on his telegram being sent to Washington, a polite and assiduous male detective kept me company through the hours that seemed like years. Our letters were few, but they were opened, and no trouble taken to conceal that they had been read first. Every letter that I received was from Edwin Booth, and I handed the same to the attendant officer, who, without asking, seemed to expect this privilege. He was gentle and polite, and although he followed me from room to room he tried not to let me feel myself a prisoner. His greatest annoyance seemed "that I never cried and seldom spoke." He was frequently urging me "to let his wife, who actually cried to think how ill-treated and sick I was, come and stay with me."

"*You* were ordered here by the Government, were you not?" I asked.

"Yes, ma'am, but *she* can come just as well, and I needn't."

"Obey your orders," I said, "but tell your wife I thank her very kindly."

I should rather have been watched by ten men who could keep quiet, than one chattering female.

Edwin Booth wrote frequently to me. From one of his letters the following paragraphs are taken. "Think no more of him as your brother; he is dead to us now, as he soon must be to all the world, but imagine the boy you loved to be in that better part of his spirit, in another world." And, "I have had a heartbroken letter from the poor little girl to whom he had promised so much happiness."

A fearful day! T. J. Hemphill of the Walnut Street Theatre asked to see me. The old man stood steadying himself by the center table; he did not raise his eyes, his face was very pale and working nervously. The attitude and pallor told the news he had been deputed to convey.

"Is it over?"

"Yes, madam."

"Taken?"

"Yes."

"Dead?"

"Yes, madam."

My heart beat like strong machinery, powerful and loud it seemed. I lay down with my face to the wall, thanking God silently, and heard the old man's sobs choking him, heard him go out, and close the street door after him.

Someone sent up, by my servant, a slip from a newspaper with the announcement that "on hearing the news Mrs. J. S. Clarke had gone mad, and was at present confined at the Asylum at West Philadelphia." North, East and West the papers teemed with the most preposterous adventures, and eccentricities, and ill deeds of the vile Booth family. The tongue of every man and woman was free to revile and insult us. Every man's hand was against us. If we had friends they condoled with us in secret; none ventured near. Keeping silent, with the thorn pressed deep, the fury died out in its vehemence. Those who have passed through such an ordeal—if there are any such— may be quick to forgive, slow to resent; they never relearn to trust in human nature, they never resume their old place in the world and they forget only in death.

Among much cruelty and unkindness, the falling off of tried friends, the terror of truculent acquaintances, the device of a young actor named Claud Burroughs*, who came on "a secret mission from Edwin Booth to demand of me, in utter secrecy, *knowledge of the paper which I had placed in my bosom,*" the later offer from John S. Clarke, for me to consent to a divorce "which would be *his* only salvation now," the fear of my

---

*Claude Burroughs (1848?—1876), in 1865 an attache at Edwin Booth's Winter Garden Theatre; later an actor.

old doctor to approach my house, the insults of the engaged monthly nurse, and her refusal to attend me—all these and more were doubly, trebly outweighed by the one true womanly letter copied below. The original is treasured as precious gold.

May 3rd, 1865,
Phila.

Mrs. Clarke,
    Dear Madam,
    Although a perfect stranger to you, I take the liberty of offering my sympathy and aid to you in your great sorrow and sickness. If my mother or myself can be of the slightest use to you in any way in this world we should be only too happy. I should have offered before, but illness prevented. May God help and bless you is the
        Constant prayer of

EFFIE GERMON*
1129 Race Street.

There is no solidity in love, no truth in friendship, no steadiness in marital faith, and no reason in an angry nation, but above and beyond all this exceeding bitterness, this little token of rare and unsought friendliness is sufficient to set the faithlessness of the world aside, and almost revive belief in human goodness.

After a lapse of many years I spoke of Claud Burroughs to Edwin Booth. He declared, in fearful surprise, "that he *never* sent Burroughs or any other actor, or any human being, to my house, on any mission, or with any message whatsoever." It is as sad to prove that glib-tongued fair-haired young actor only a detective in disguise, as it was delightful to know that beautiful actress a warm, true-hearted woman.

---

*Effie Germon (1843?—1914), star actor who had performed with Booth in 1863.

Junius Booth, Sr., father of John Wilkes Booth, c. 1847

Mary Ann Booth, mother of John Wilkes Booth, in previously unpublished photograph, c. 1865

Tudor Hall, the Booth home, near Bel Air, Maryland, shown in 1865. A neighborhood family, unrelated to the Booths, poses on porch. (courtesy of Preservation Association of Tudor Hall)

All photographs are from the editor's collection unless otherwise indicated.

Edwin Booth, elder brother of John Wilkes Booth

John Wilkes Booth, rising young star of the stage, during Civil War

Junius Brutus Booth, Jr., actor and eldest brother of John Wilkes Booth (courtesy of Jonathan Mann)

Asia Booth, c. 1850s
(courtesy of
Putnam Publish-
ing Group)

John S. Clarke, husband of Asia
Booth (courtesy of Richard and
Kellie Gutman Collection)

John Wilkes Booth, at about twenty, in one
of the earliest known photographs

John Wilkes Booth, as he appears at the height of his stage career during the Civil War

John Wilkes Booth, tempted by Satan, as he appears to an artist after the assassination, 1865

Edwin Booth's letters at this sad time were filled by re-
iterated suggestions for "Clarke to dissolve all partnership
with him." *He* must not be bound in any way to him whose
"name and fame were irremediably clouded. He must sever
all connection with him, theatrically and for ever now." This
was a generous offer, made when he, Edwin Booth had all
the world against him; but he little knew how ungenerous an
offer John S. Clarke was about to make to one whom he had
sworn to keep faithful to under more solemn bonds than those
of *business*. The incomprehensible words of Wilkes Booth
resounded through the years that followed this astounding,
heart-sickening proposition: "Bear in mind that you are only a
professional stepping-stone."

Amid the happy scenes of our childhood the sensation hunt-
ers were actively entertained. There was no surfeit, and Stephen Hooper, the negro, gave valuable testimony of the "doin's
of the Booths at the farms." The trench, in which a boy and
girl had dug with unremitting toil through the best time of a
summer vacation to find a dead Indian chief and relics, was
made to appear as an underground store for secreted arms
and ammunition. The Hallowe'en raid, although the custom of
the country, was exaggerated into "frequent robberies of fowls,
cattle and grain by which the idle Booth family were sustained,
rather than do a stroke of honest work." Our near neighbor
vouched for "the cruelty of Wilkes, who had destroyed valuable
game and marketable fowl, destroyed innocent dogs and wild
creatures for sport"—nothing was safe that came within range
of his gun. He had left for dead a workman whom he had
battered with a club, etc., etc. Then, another swore that "the
visits of old Ishmael Day"* (who had become a hero of the
North) "were only made to try and discover what we rebels
were up to, and not for friendship's sake as we supposed." In
that time there were no rebels, for there had been no war [yet],

---

*Ishmael Day, an elderly Maryland farmer who achieved public notice when
he killed a rebel soldier during a Confederate cavalry raid in 1864.

but untruth and memory seldom go twinned, and old Ishmael Day had been a casual visitor to the farm before the birth of Wilkes Booth or the young members of our father's family. He was a strange man, with some curse or shame upon him, as he thought, but we regarded him with respect and received him with politeness always.

What is herein written, to be read after my death, is the truth so far as I have been able to understand it, or to transcribe it. That my husband J. S. Clarke was entirely innocent, by knowledge or complicity, in any design whatsoever with Wilkes Booth, no one who ever knew the two men could for an instant doubt. Their temperaments, ideas, dispositions, natures, were widely at variance. The too careless guardian of his own household, being of a heavy, lymphatic temperament, yet to those who mean kindly, his indifference and utter apathy might appear "unsuspecting innocence of evil." Wilkes was an entirely opposite creation. They had no tie in common beyond the accidental one of a marriage connection. That my husband went to prison to save me is a fallacious assertion. The very fact of the summons, and the doctor's certificate for inability, disproves it. Suspicion was directed to his house through the unwise publication of a letter said to have been "secreted on the premises" (but which I promptly and freely produced, reserving to myself the right of destroying a written name that I would have suffered death rather than expose). Probably without this we should have remained untouched, as did Edwin Booth. This latter was an upright honest man, espousing the Northern policy, and had cast his vote for Abraham Lincoln. J. B. Booth and Joseph Booth were neutral.

I loved my brothers devotedly, but Wilkes had grown nearer in those late years at the farm, where we were lonely together. My marriage, which he often urged me to free myself from, was become less pleasing to him; this and his professional pursuits separated us at long intervals. He was prudent not to trust me too far, yet he knew that I loved the Marylanders as dearly as himself. Many, many of our young friends had gone down in that unholy war. We glorified Washington and believed in the Constitution. We had many tastes, ideas, and loves in common, but he never even trusted me enough to disclose the whereabouts or meaning of Michael O'Laughlin. Romance and sentiment were woven in those days, and friendships, but no one is the worse for having loved and believed. In the darkness we are happier for once having known the blessing of sight, and the memory of youth is sweet in age. Wilkes never hinted at a scheme, or plot, or any design, legal or illegal. Revenge was a word I never heard from his lips, and I heard many hard epithets for those who tried to subjugate the South. The story of "the bullet which he carried" was concocted at our house, at our table. The origin of it was, "I suppose he was mad enough to carry a bullet in his pocket, with the man's name engraved upon it." This bitter wit was repeated, by lip, and then by pen, and ere long the bullet, so engraved, had been *seen* in different cities, by different persons, who each swore to the truth of the story, and repeated the threat and their conversations with Wilkes.

He who talks loudly of suicide and murder never carries his threats into effect. The thinker is the plotter and the worker; danger is silent. If it cried aloud there would be no danger. Those men, and they are yet increasing in number, who knew him to write his victim's name upon a window pane, and who talked with him while he displayed that famous bullet, were more guilty than he, for either act proclaimed him a madman or themselves accomplices. His was a strongly defined character; looking through all his years it shows consistency. He was a man who could keep a secret, was never a loquacious guest, and was considered abstemious and temperate. The diamond writing on the window glass emanated from the same prolific wit that lashed with scorpions but could do nothing openly.

The little volume of the "Memoir of Booth the Elder" was hurriedly written and arranged for publication in a few months of mental and bodily anguish. It was ready for the press before the 20th of August, 1865, on which day the sad writer gave birth to two babes.

Edwin Booth made several vain requests for possession of his brother's body. The answer was *"to wait,"* but the belief of the family and of all interested in the matter was that he had been buried at sea.

Wilkes Booth was not insane; he had a powerful and active brain, and was given to weigh his intents and reflect upon his actions. "Trust to luck is cheerful enough for a song, but I trust to my brains," he said. His was a developed character in boyhood. He did not change much as he matured, only his opinions and principles became more riveted and his friendships stronger. He seldom chattered for pastime, but generally meant what he cared to utter. There are those who judge that men and women who can keep silence, and preserve secrets entrusted to them, are evil essentially, in mind and soul. John S. Clarke abhorred the "secretiveness of the whole Booth race." To his way of thinking it stamped them [as] male and female Iagos. That may be in some measure a truth, and I less than any care to vindicate my character on that score, but my observation has convinced me that Mr. J. S. Clarke's mistakes, which are few, have been the result of a merry and over-indulged loquacity.

Contrasting [Wilkes'] deeds with his peaceful domestic qualities, there seems to have been the impetus of a desperate fate impelling him. We make our destinies, perhaps, but is not each one known to God, and may not the gloom foreshadow us in a greater or lesser degree as our lives partake of sorrow, even as the shadow of the Cross hung over Jesus?

These old diaries keep many trivial records of Wilkes that would sound like fulsome praise. Let another speak of his warm heart and generous nature; there must be those who will do so in fitting time, for he had crowds of friends. The doom that fell on him was not wrought from a maniac brain nor a wicked heart, not from an irreligious soul nor a degraded nature. I believe that with the kidnaping scheme was laid to rest, although with curses, the cherished hope of saving those he would have died to serve. But the fall of Richmond rang in with maddening, exasperating clang of joy, and that triumphant entry into the fallen city (which was not magnanimous) breathed air afresh upon the fire which consumed him.

It was the moan of the religious people, the one throb of anguish to hero-worshipers, that the President had not gone first to a place of worship or have remained at home on this jubilant occasion. It desecrated his idea to have his end come in a devil's den—a theater—in fact. Conquerors cannot be too careful of themselves, as history has ever proved. That fatal visit to the theater had no pity in it; it was jubilation over fields of unburied dead, over miles of desolated homes. It was neither the Te Deum of a noble conqueror nor the Miserere of a Christian nation. It struck the keynote for re-election and re-elections unnumbered. It was defying Washington, contemning the Constitution. It meant to him, to this one desperate man who shouted "Sic semper tyrannis," the fall of the Republic, a dynasty of kings. When he lay dying fast, outside the barn at Bowling Green, the last words uttered, between great gasps for breath, were his will and testament; so firmly did he believe in what he had done, that he declared with his departing strength, "Tell my mother—I died—for my country!"

"He saved his country from a king," but he created for her a martyr. And yet the word *martyr* signifies one who suffers and dies for a belief and a cause. He set the stamp of greatness on an epoch of history, and gave all he had to build this enduring monument to his foe. We regard Boston Corbett[*] as our deliverer, for by his shot he saved our beloved brother from an ignominious death. He by *his* act gave to his country her first martyr, and to history a hero who would blush to recognize his own posthumous greatness.

---

[*]Boston Corbett (1832—?), New York cavalryman who fired the shot which killed Booth at Garrett's farm on April 26, 1865.

I returned Boston Corbett's letter to him; he did not request it exactly, but I thought it honorable to do so and safer at the time not to retain it. I kept a copy of my reply to it. He is still living, but I know he is not happy. He is a brave man and an enthusiast. May he have no regret.

The South avenged the wrongs inflicted by the North. A life inexpressibly dear was sacrificed wildly for what its possessor deemed best. The life best beloved by the North was dashed madly out when most triumphant. Let the blood of both cement the indissoluble union of our country. Slavery is over, white labor omnipotent. Boston Corbett lies without a monument, they tell me, for he is dead now. The North has not immortalized this hero, she had too many perhaps.

If Wilkes Booth was mad, his mind lost its balance between the fall of Richmond and the terrific end. The world will arise from its torpor of hatred. The light of reason will show that success alone makes the hero or the outlaw. It were ill to extol his action, as to debase his motive; they were the offspring of his own brain, the creatures of his own terrible will. Both are amenable to a higher justice. But, granting that he died in vain, yet he gave his all on earth, youth, beauty, manhood, a great human love, the certainty of excellence in his profession, a powerful brain, the strength of an athlete, health and great wealth, for "*his cause*." This man was noble in his life, he periled his immortal soul, and he was brave in death. Already his hidden remains are given Christian burial, and strangers have piled his grave with flowers.

"So runs the world away."*

ASIA BOOTH-CLARKE

1874

---

*Hamlet, act 3, scene 2.

FAMILY LETTERS
AND DOCUMENTS

John Wilkes Booth's Farewell Letter To His Mother and His "To Whom It May Concern" Letter

These two documents were discovered on Sunday, April 16, 1865, by Booth's mother, sister Asia and brother-in-law Clarke in a safe at the Clarke home in Philadelphia. It has not been possible to determine precisely when they were written. According to the statement given to authorities by Clarke when he was a prisoner in Washington, Booth left a package of papers at his home for safekeeping in late November, 1864. Booth retrieved and returned the package (or one like it) in January, 1865. A chronology of his abduction plotting, together with certain internal clues in the documents, suggest the letters were written at the former date.

Farewell Letter to His Mother

Booth's devotion to his widowed mother was noted by many of his personal and theatrical friends. Even while dying on the porch of the Garrett farmhouse in Virginia on April 26, 1865, he spoke her name among his last words. This letter is an additional indication of his affection for her. And it shows his distress at withdrawing his promise of 1861 to stay clear of the war. The letter, whose publication was suppressed at the time, was thought lost for many years. In 1977 historian James

O. Hall located it at the National Archives among the records of Attorney General James Speed.

1. *John Wilkes Booth to Mary Ann Booth*[1]

[No place given]
[November, 1864?]

Dearest Beloved Mother,

Heaven knows how dearly I love you, and may our kind Father in Heaven (if only for the sake of my love) watch over, comfort, and protect you in my absence. May he soften the blow of my departure, granting you peace and happiness for many, many years to come. God ever bless you.

I have always endeavored to be a good and dutiful son, and even now would wish to die sooner than give you pain. But, dearest Mother, though I owe you all, there is another duty, a noble duty, for the sake of liberty and humanity due to my country. For four years I have lived (I may say) a *slave* in the North (a favored slave it's true, but no less hateful to me on that account), not daring to express my thoughts or sentiments, even in my own home, constantly hearing every principle dear to my heart denounced as treasonable, and knowing the vile and savage acts committed on my countrymen, their wives, and helpless children, that I have cursed my wilful idleness, and begun to deem myself a coward and to despise my own existence. For four years I have borne it mostly for your dear sake, and for you alone have I struggled to fight off this desire to be gone, but it seems that uncontrollable fate, moving me for its ends, takes me from you, dear Mother, to do what work I can for a poor, oppressed, downtrodden people. May that same fate cause me to do that work well. I care not for the censure of the North, so I have your forgiveness, and I feel I may hope it, even though you differ with me in opinion.

I may, by the grace of God, live through this war, dear Mother; and if so the rest of my life shall be more devoted to you than has my former, for I know it will take a long lifetime of tenderness and care to atone for the pang this parting will give you. But I cannot longer resist the inclination to go and share the sufferings of my brave countrymen, holding an unequal strife (for every right human and divine) against the most ruthless enemy the world has ever known. You can answer for me, dearest Mother (although none of you think with me) that I have not a *single selfish motive* to spur me on to this. Nothing save the sacred duty I feel I owe the cause I love, the cause of the South, the cause of liberty and justice. So should I meet the *worst*, dear Mother, in struggling for such holy rights, I can say "God's will be done," and bless him in my heart for not permitting me to outlive our dear bought freedom, and for keeping me from being longer a hidden lie among my country's foes.

Darling Mother, I cannot write you. You will understand the deep regret, the forsaking your dear side, will make me suffer, for you have been the best, the noblest, an example for all Mothers. God, God bless you, as I shall ever pray him to do. And should the last *bolt* strike your son, dear Mother, bear it patiently and think at the best life is short, and *not at all times happy.* My Brothers and Sisters (Heaven protect them) will add my love and duty to their own, and watch you with care and kindness, till we meet again. And if *that happiness* does not come to us on earth, then may, O may it be with God. So then, dearest, *dearest* Mother, *forgive* and pray for me. I feel that I am right in the justness of my cause, and that we shall, *ere long*, meet again. Heaven grant it. Bless you, bless you. Your loving son will never cease to hope and pray for such a joy.

Come weal or woe, with never ending love and devotion, you will find me ever, your affectionate son
John.

THE "TO WHOM IT MAY CONCERN" LETTER

This letter, dated only with the year 1864, sets forth Booth's views of the North-South struggle as the Civil War entered its final six months. It takes its title from a phrase in an opening paragraph addressed by Booth to an unnamed "Dear Sir." The publication of the letter in the *Philadelphia Inquirer* of April 19, 1865, was authorized by U. S. Marshal William Millward. He felt the letter would show the public that Booth "was not only the assassin, but that he had acted in concert with others as a member of an extended and diabolical conspiracy. . . ." While the letter does not actually support Millward's claim of a widespread plot against Lincoln, it does show that Booth was passionate in his Southern views.

Denounced as fake by a writer in the *Washington Chronicle*, the letter was genuine enough and quickly reprinted in newspapers throughout the North. "A Secession Rhapsody" was the headline given the letter by the *Inquirer*. As such it was received in the North. William Seymour, an actor who had known and performed with Booth, wrote years later, "The signs of insanity are in this letter."

2. *The "To Whom It May Concern" Letter*[2]

[No place]
[November?], 1864

My dear Sir,

You may use this, as you think best. But as *some may* wish to know *when, who and why* and know not *how* to direct, I give it (In the words of your master [Abraham Lincoln])

"To whom it may concern."

Right or wrong, God judge me, not man. For be my motive good or bad, of one thing I am sure, the lasting condemnation of the North.

I love peace more than life. Have loved the Union beyond expression. For four years have I waited, hoped and prayed, for the dark clouds to break, and for a restoration of our former sunshine. To wait longer would be a crime. All hope for peace is dead. My prayers have proved as idle as my hopes. God's will be done. I go to see, and share the bitter end.

I have ever held the South were right. The very nomination of Abraham Lincoln four years ago, spoke plainly, war—war upon Southern rights and institutions. His election proved it. "Await an overt act." Yes, until you are bound and plundered. What folly. The South were wise. Who thinks of argument or patience when the finger of his enemy presses on the trigger. In a *foreign war,* I too could say 'Country right or wrong,' but in a struggle *such as ours* (where the brother tries to pierce the brother's heart) for God's sake choose the right. When a country like this spurns *justice* from her side, she forfeits the allegiance of every honest freeman, and should leave him, untrammeled by any fealty soever, to act as his conscience may approve.

People of the North, to hate tyranny, to love liberty and justice, to strike at wrong and oppression, was the teaching of our fathers. The study of our early history will not let *me* forget it. And may it never.

This country was formed for the *white*, not for the black man. And looking upon *African slavery* from the same standpoint held by those noble framers of our Constitution, I for one have ever considered *it* one of the greatest blessings (both for themselves and us) that God ever bestowed upon a favored nation. Witness heretofore our wealth and power. Witness their elevation in happiness and enlightenment above their race elsewhere. I have lived among it most of my life and have seen *less* harsh treatment from master to man than I have beheld in the North from father to son. Yet, Heaven knows *no one* would be willing to do *more* for the negro race than I, could I but see a way to still *better their* condition. But Lincoln's policy is only preparing the way for their total annihilation.

The South *are not nor have they been fighting* for the continuance of slavery. The first battle of Bull-run did away with that idea. Their causes *since* for *war* have been as *noble*, and *greater far, than those that urged our fathers on. Even* should we allow they were *wrong* at the beginning of this contest, *cruelty and injustice* have made the wrong become the *right*. And they stand *now* (before the wonder and admiration of the *world*) as a noble band of patriotic heroes. Hereafter, reading of *their deeds,* Thermoplyae will be forgotten.

When I aided in the capture and execution of John Brown (who was a murderer on our Western Border, and who was fairly *tried* and *convicted,*—before an impartial judge & jury— of treason—and who by the way has since been made a God [)]—I was proud of my little share in the transaction, for I deemed it my duty and that I was helping our common country to perform an act of justice. But what was a crime in poor John Brown is now considered (by themselves) as the greatest and only virtue, of the whole Republican party. Strange transmigra- tion. *Vice* to become a *virtue* simply because *more* indulge in it.

I thought then, *as now,* that the abolitionists *were the only traitors* in the land, and that the entire party deserved the fate of poor old Brown, not because they wish to abolish slavery, but on account of the means they have ever endeavored to use to effect that abolition. If Brown were living, I doubt if he *himself* would set slavery against the Union. Most, or many, in the North do, and openly curse the Union if the South are to return and retain a *single right* guaranteed them by every tie which we once *revered as sacred.* The South can make no choice. It is either extermination or slavery for *themselves* (worse than death) to draw from. I would know *my* choice.

I have, also, studied hard to discover upon what grounds the right of a state to secede has been denied, when our very name (United States) and our Declaration of Independence, *both* provide for secession. But there is no time for words. I write in haste.

I know how foolish I shall be deemed, for undertaking such a step as this, where on the one side I have many friends and everything to make me happy. Where my profession *alone* has gained me an income of *more than* twenty thousands dollars a year. And where my great personal ambition in my profession has such a great field for labor. On the other hand the South have never bestowed upon me one kind word; a place now where I have no friends except beneath the sod; a place where I must either become a private soldier or a beggar. To give up all of the *former* for the *latter*, besides my mother and sisters whom I love so dearly (although they so widely differ with me in opinion) seems insane. But God is my judge. I love *justice* more than I do a country that disowns it, more than fame and wealth, more (Heaven pardon me if wrong), more than a happy home.

I have never been upon a battle-field, but O my countrymen, could you all but see the *reality* or effects of this horrid war, as I have seen them (in *every state*, save Virginia) I know you would think like me and would pray the Almighty to create in the Northern mind a sense of *right* and *justice* (even should it possess no seasoning of mercy) and that he would dry up the sea of blood between us which is daily growing wider.

Alas, poor country, is she to meet her threatened doom. Four years ago I would have given a thousand lives to see her remain (as I had always known her) powerful and unbroken. And even now I would hold my life as naught to see her what she was. O my friends if the fearful scenes of the past four years had never been enacted, or if what has been had been but a frightful dream from which we could now awake, with what overflowing hearts could we bless our God and pray for his continued favor. How I have loved the *old flag* can never, now, be known. A few years since and the entire world could boast of *none* so pure and spotless. But I have of late been seeing and hearing of the *bloody deeds* of which she has *been made the emblem*, and would shudder to think how changed she had grown. O how I have longed to see her break from the mist of blood and death that circles round her folds, spoiling her beauty and tarnishing her honor. But no, day by day has she been draged [*sic*] deeper and deeper into cruelty and oppression, till now (in my eyes) her once bright red stripes look like *bloody gashes* on the face of Heaven. I look now upon my early admiration of her glories as a dream.

My love (as things stand today) is for the South alone. Nor do I deem it a dishonor, in attempting to make for her a prisoner of this man to whom she owes so much of misery. If success attends me, I go penniless to her side. They say she has found *that* "last ditch" which the North have so long derided and been endeavoring to force her in, forgetting they are our brothers and that it's impolitic to goad an enemy to madness. Should I reach her in safety and find it true, I will proudly beg permission to triumph or die in that same "ditch" by her side.

A *Confederate, ~~at present~~* * *doing duty upon his own responsibility.*

J. Wilkes Booth

---

*Deleted in the original by Booth.

THE BOOTH FAMILY

The following documents have never before been collected together and published. They contain accounts made by members of the Booth family relating to John Wilkes Booth and his assassination of President Abraham Lincoln. The documents make compelling reading. They illuminate more fully the closing months of John's life. They also show the personal dilemmas of his family members. The Booths, in common with the great majority of other Northerners, were shocked at Lincoln's murder. But unique to them was the bewilderment, turmoil, and disgrace of being related to the assassin. For all their peculiarities and feuds the Booths were an unusually close family. Their pain at being thrust into the fiery furnace of history is clear.

EDWIN BOOTH

John's older brother Edwin Booth had begun his theatrical career in 1849 as an assistant to his father. After several challenging years in California, he had returned to the eastern states in 1856 and began a steady climb upwards in the profession. He was a top dramatic actor by the time of the Civil War. The evening of April 14, 1865, found him performing in Boston. He returned quickly to his home in New York City. Unlike Junius B. Booth, Jr., Joseph Booth, and John S. Clarke, he was not arrested, although authorities did escort him to Washington, D.C., during the trial of John's fellow conspirators when it appeared his testimony might be needed. In the postwar years Edwin became one of the greatest actors of his generation.

1. *Edwin Booth to Henry C. Jarrett, manager of the Boston Theatre.*[3]

Franklin Square
Boston
April 15, 1865

My dear Sir,

With the deepest sorrow and great agitation, I thank you for relieving me from my engagement with yourself and the public. The news of the morning has made me wretched indeed, not only because I have received the unhappy tidings of the suspicion of a brother's crime, but because a good man and a most justly honored and patriotic ruler has fallen in an hour of National joy by the hand of an assassin.

The memory of the thousands who have fallen on the field in our country's defence during this struggle cannot be forgotten by me even in this, the most distressing day of my life. And I most sincerely pray that the victories we have already won may stay the hand of war and the tide of loyal blood.

While mourning in common with all other loyal hearts the death of the President, I am oppressed by a private woe not to be expressed in words. But whatever calamity may befall me or mine, my country one and indivisible, has my warmest devotion.

Edwin Booth

2. *Edwin Booth to Adam Badeau*[4]

[Boston]
April 16, [1865]

My dear Ad,

For the first time since the damnable intelligence stunned me [that my brother Wilkes enacted this fearful, hellish deed] am I able to write and hasten to acquaint you of my existence as it has been so long a time since I last wrote you, making me afraid [of] my silence. You know Ad, how I have labored since dear Mary* was called from me to establish a name that my child and all my friends wd. be proud of; you know how I have always toiled for the comfort & welfare of my family— though in vain, as well you know, how loyal I have been from the first moment of this damned rebellion, and you must feel deeply the agony I bear in being thus blasted in all my hopes [by a villain who seemed so loveable and in whom all his family found a source of joy in his boyish and confiding nature].

Alas! how frightful is the spectacle, what shall become of me. . . . Poor Mother! I go to New York to day—expecting to find her either dead or dying. I've remained here thus long at the advice of friends who thought it necessary that I shd. be set right before the public of Boston to whom I owe so much of all that is dear to me.—You know our friends who loved & appreciated my Mary so well and as many who have ever been—even in this most awful hour my firm and staunch friends.

Abraham Lincoln was my President for in pure admiration of his noble career & Christian principles I did what I never did before—I *voted* & for him! I was two days ago one of the happiest men alive—Grant's magnificent work accomplished . . . and sweet Peace turning her radiant face again upon our country.

Now what am I? Oh! how little did I dream, my boy, when on Friday night I was as Sir Edward Mortimer exclaiming, "Where is my honor now?" that I was not acting but uttering the fearful truth.

I have a great deal to tell you of myself & the beautiful plans I had for the future—all blasted now, but must wait until my mind is more settled. I am half crazy now—You will be pleased to know that the deepest sympathy is expressed for me here—and by none more sincerely than dear old Gov. [John A.] Andrew [of Massachusetts].

God bless you,

Ned

---

*Mary Devlin Booth, Edwin's wife who died in 1863. They had one child, a daughter Edwina, born in 1861.

3. *Edwin Booth to Mrs. John B. Murray*[5]

[New York, N.Y.]
[April 27, 1865]

My dear Mrs. Murray,

At last the terrible end is known [the death of John]—fearful as it is, it is notwithstanding a blessed relief.

Poor Mother was telegraphed for & started in the 11 1/2 train—learning the news of her boy's fate on the ferry-boat.

Junius' arrest on suspicion does not trouble me more than the abuse & the added disgrace (if there can be more than what is already heaped upon us) to our poor house.

Pardon me for troubling you—but I am at a loss what to do—but thought I would seek advice from Mr. Murray before I took any steps in the matter. Whether I had better go on or remain here—I am afraid of obeying my own heart & my head is too confused to guide me.

Will you be kind enough to send Mr. Murray to me when he returns from his business? Something tells me that I must be found at home—and yet my heart bids me go to those who are in need of some one stronger and calmer than they can be.

Pray forgive this interview—the great goodness I have received at your hands assured me that I shall find what I seek now.

Most faithfully
Yr. Servt.
Edwin Booth

4. *Edwin Booth to Emma F. Cary*[6]

[New York City]
May 6, 1865

My Dear Friend,

I've just received y'r letter. I have been in one sense unable to write, but you know, of course, what my condition is, and need no excuses.

I have been, by the advice of my friends, 'cooped up' since I arrived here, going out only occasionally in the evening. My health is good, but I suffer from the want of fresh air and exercise.

Poor mother is in Philadelphia, about crushed by her sorrows, and my sister, Mrs. Clarke, is ill and without the least knowledge of her husband, who was taken from her several days ago, with Junius.

My position is such a delicate one that I am obliged to use the utmost caution. Hosts of friends are staunch and true to me, here and in Boston. I feel safe. What I am in Phila. and elsewhere I know not. All I do [know] of the above named city [of Philadelphia] is that there is one great heart, firm and faster bound to me than ever.[*] Sent in answer to dear Mary's prayers, I faithfully believe. She will do what Mary struggled, suffered, and died in doing.

My baby, too, is there.[†] Now that the greatest excitement is over, and a lull is in the storm, I feel the need of that dear angel; but during the heat of it I was glad she was not here.

When Junius and Mr. Clarke are at liberty, mother will come here and bring Edwina to me.

I wish I could see with others' eyes; all my friends assure me that my name shall be free and that in a little while I may be where I was and what I was; but, alas! it looks dark to me.

God bless you all for your great assistance in my behalf; even dear Dick aided me in my extremity, did he not?

Give my love to all and kisses to Georgie. . . . I do not think the feeling is so strong in my favor in Phila. as it is here and in Boston. I am not known there. . . .

Ever yours,
Edwin Booth

---

[*]Blanche Hanel, Edwin's fiancée who lived in Philadelphia.
[†]Emma's brother, Capt. Richard Cary, killed in 1862.

5. Edwin Booth to Nahum Capen[7]

Windsor Hotel
[London]
July 28, 1881

Dear Sir,

I can give you very little information regarding my brother John. I seldom saw him since his early boyhood in Baltimore.

He was a rattle-pated fellow, filled with Quixotic notions. While at the farm in Maryland, he would charge on horseback through the woods, 'spouting' heroic speeches with a lance in his hand, a relic of the Mexican war, given to father by some soldier who had served under Taylor.

We regarded him as a good-hearted, harmless, though wild-brained boy, and used to laugh at his patriotic froth whenever secession was discussed. That he was insane on that one point, no one who knew him well can doubt.

When I told him that I had voted for Lincoln's re-election, he expressed deep regret, and declared his belief that Lincoln would be made king of America; and this, I believe, drove him beyond the limits of reason.

I asked him once why he did not join the Confederate army. To which he replied: "I promised mother I would keep out of the quarrel, if possible, and I am sorry that I said so."

Knowing my sentiments, he avoided me, rarely visiting my house, except to see his mother, when political topics were not touched upon, at least in my presence.

He was of a gentle, loving disposition, very boyish and full of fun—his mother's darling,—and his deed and death crushed her spirit.

He possessed rare dramatic talent, and would have made a brilliant mark in the theatrical world.

This is positively all that I know about him, having left him a mere schoolboy when I went with my father to California in 1852. On my return in '56 we were separated by professional engagements, which kept him mostly in the South, while I was employed in the Eastern and Northern States.

I do not believe any of the wild, romantic stories in the papers concerning him; but of course he may have been engaged in political matters of which I know nothing. All his theatrical friends speak of him as a poor, crazy boy, and such his family think of him.

I am sorry I can afford you no further light on the subject.

> Very truly yours,
> Edwin Booth

JUNIUS BRUTUS BOOTH, JR.

Seventeen years older than John Wilkes Booth, "June" Booth was away from home pursuing his own career in distant cities when his younger brother was growing up. His rare visits to the farm were delightful to John. The athletic June spent hours with the boy, teaching him to fence and to box. After a lengthy residence in California, June returned to the eastern states in 1864. Politically neutral, he was fond of this brother above others and very attached to him.

Junius would return to the theater subsequently as an actor and manager.

1. *Junius B. Booth, Jr., to Edwin Booth*[8]

> Ph[iladelphi]a
> [April 24, 1865]

Dear Brother,

I recd. yours this morning—words of consolation are idle—we must use philosophy. 'Tis a mere matter of time. The grief & shame of this blow will pass away—human pride must always be liable to fall—but our fall has been heavy. Time is the only cure for our ills & I feel sure Time will bring all things right—that is, as right as we have any right to expect.

But poor Mother, who can console her, for a mother is a mother ever, and I am afraid she can never be brought to look calmly on this dreadful calamity. I have written to Mother &

what I have said to her, I could only repeat to you. I want you to read it & have requested her to give it to you.

Blanche [Hanel] called today. I did not see her, but Asia had a long talk with her & all seems right.

God bless you, dear brother. I have warned Mother about Sharpers who wish to get money—see that she holds no communication with weeping imposters.

All well. Again, God bless you.

Yours ever,

June

[P.S.] Write more legibly, for some of your last neither John [S. Clarke], Asia or myself can read. You say you write in haste—don't hurry.

2. *"Statement of J. B. Booth"*[9]

[Washington, D.C.]

May 5, 1865

After an absence of ten years in Califa., I returned to the East & saw J. Wilkes Booth for the 1st time since '54 & was sorry to find him so strongly sympathizing with the Southern cause. I endeavored by every argument I was possessed of to [present] a different view of the subject & we had many & long arguments on the question.

My brother Edwin & brother in law C. [*sic*] S. Clarke would not argue with him for they considered him a monomaniac on the subject & not worth while arguing with. So did I but felt my duty as an elder brother to do all I could & prove to him that the government was doing its duty. That a southern independent nation would be the ruin of the whole United States &c. He would listen but would not change his ideas. I told him the Civil War was but a large family quarrel & would in a few years be made up & peace be restored. In all my letters to him it alluded to its being a family quarrel & I begged him to keep clear of it for I always feared he might join the South 'tho he promised me often that he would not for his Mother's

& his family sake & expressed much gratitude for the interest I took in his welfare & said he would make me a present of some oil stock (for he was much interested in oil speculations).

About this time, the latter part of the month of August, he had a severe family quarrel on politics. [*Deleted from statement*: After that politics were never debated in the house.]

I & Edwin went to Pha. on the 1st of Sept. & J. W. Booth went to Canada as he said to play an Eng[agemen]t. I did not see him again untill [*sic*] the day of the Presidential Election where I met him in Balt. on my return from Washington. All his talk then was buying farms cheap on the potomac & wanted to form a Co[mpany] to buy up the land now, for it could be got for much less than its value. That & oil was all his conversation, for [he] had ceased to argue with me on politics for neither could convince the other.

We went on to NY together & played at the Winter Garden Theatre for one night. He immediately after departed for Washington which from [this?] time he seemed to make his home, only coming to see the family for a day or two at long intervals—on a few of which I saw him. He said he was forming an oil Co. in Washington & could do better by it than by acting & we all believed him.

In Feb. [1865] I went to Washington & was informed that he had played one night in a borrowed dress & when I questioned him about not wearing his own, he said he had left his wardrobe in Canada. Afterwards I found some contradiction in his statements & after questioning him close[ly] he confessed that after the the [*sic*] quarrel aluded [*sic*] to in August that he went to Canada & shipped his wardrobe to the South meaning to play there for the future—that he had disposed of most of his property in gifts for he did not mean to take anything he had made in the North but to go there & act & commence the world anew—but that the vessel had been sunk by a gun boat & his wardrobe was lost. So he had now given up the idea of going South & that was [illegible] as he had no wardrobe, he could not act. So [he] had turned all his attention to the oil business in which he was doing well. I believed him as did everyone who knew him in Washington. I was thankful that his wardrobe was lost & hoped that he had given up all thoughts of going South. He assured me he had.

The next day I left for Pha. & did not see him again till about Feb. 11 when he stopped in Pha. for one day & left for NY where I saw him on the 14th as I passed through the city on my way to Boston. On my return he had left for Washington. I was then informed that he was not making as much money by oil as he had represented in Washington but was losing fine opportunities by not being in the oil regions—Venango C[oun]ty, Pen.

The next & last time I saw him was in the last week of March when he came to NY for a few days. I then told him what I had read about his wasting his time in Washington when he could do so much better in the oil counties. He said it was true but that he would not live in the oil regions for all the wealth in them & that he was in love with a lady in Washington [Lucy Hale] & that was worth more to him than all the money he could make. He only staid [*sic*] in NY a couple of days & returned to Washington.

I went to Cincinnati where I had an Engt. Ap. 2. On Wed., Apl. 12 I recd. a letter from him from NY saying that he had been to Boston & in a day or so would go to Washington. The letter was only a few lines, saying that he had given me some oil stock & tho' not worth much now he had no doubt it would be valuable in a short time & advising me not to sell it—that he hoped soon to see me in NY.

This letter I recd. late in the afternoon of Wed. [April] 12 & as I had only a few moments to spare before going to the theatre, wrote him a few hurried lines, thanking him for the present of the stock—that I would not sell it—that I hoped he would leave the oil bus & follow his profession, that I hoped to see him in NY on Ap 22 to play for the Shakespeare fund & that then I would go with him in to the Oil country & see the sinking of the wells there &c. That of course he had heard of the fall of Rich[mon]d, the surrender of Lee, & that the war would soon be over. I used the word of course &c. because when ever I would mention any success of the federal arms, he would say that he had not heard it—or that it was a false report &c. & would soon be corrected. I begged him to have nothing to do with family quarrels by which title I had always referred to the war or any discussion of it for I was fearful that the reverse of the South would lead him to say something he would regret, never dreaming that he would join a hopeless cause when he had refrained from doing so so long. The letter was written in a hurry but as far as I remember the above is the substance of it—with a postscript [illegible] to be remembered to a mutual lady friend.

On Friday [actually, Saturday, April 15], 10 am, I was first informed of the dreadful deed which has caused so much woe & misery to the nation & to our family in particular. I remained in Cincinnati till Monday night, feeling to [sic] distressed to travel & arrived in Pha. Wednesday Ap 19.

I immediately made know [sic] my arrival to the U. S. Marshall Millard [sic] in case my evidence or presence be wanted in Washington. I there found the oil stock to which he referred in his last letter, dated & recorded in Sept or Nov I forget which.

On Sunday [April 23] I read a garbled & false account of my letter in the papers & was about starting for Washington to enquire about it, but was dissuaded by my friends who said it might not be safe for me to travel & that the authorities knew where I could be found. On Tuesday [April 25] an officer took me to Washington.

This is a true & full statement of all I know of J. W. Booth that has anything to do with or relating to his business affairs. For myself I have always espoused the cause of the government of the U.S. & the re-election of President Lincoln. My associates have always been true & loyal men & [I] have always avoided any conversation or business transactions with those not so, both here & in Calif.

All my conversations & letters with J. W. Booth have been to make him change his views or if I could not, to implore him for his Mother & the family sake to take no part in the Rebel cause & he always promised me he would not.

What I suffer for is doing the duty of a brother & a loyal citizen in trying to prevent a friend of the South from becoming an armed Enemy of My country, while the uncontradicted assertion that I was an aider & abettor of treason is being promulgated through the land.

J. B. Booth

Subscribed & sworn
> before me May 6 /65
> L. C. Turner
> J. Advocate

3. *Junius B. Booth's Statement on the Oil Stock*[10]

[Washington, D.C.]
May 3, 1865

Junius Brutus Booth states:

I do not know what amount of oil stock my brother had. He had some stock in some company in Venango County. He wanted me to go into the oil business with him. I told him no, that I had no faith in it. That was in July or August last.

He was a third partner with a man by the name of Ellsler & a man by the name of Meers.* As I said, he wanted me to go into the oil business. I had been so unlucky in mining speculations that I said I had no faith in it. "Well," said he, "I will give you some some day." Said I, "If you do, I will take it, but I will never buy a cent's worth."

About three weeks ago, I think it was, he wrote to me saying, "I have given you some oil stock, and I do not want you to sell it because it will be good some day although it is not worth much now.["]

When I returned from Cincinnati I found a deed at the house of my brother[-in-law] in Philadelphia. I forget the date. It was

---

*John Ellsler and Thomas Meers, residents of Cleveland, were Booth's oil partners. Joseph Simonds was an oil-country friend who helped manage his business affairs.

since the murder. It was along with a lot of documents that were left there. This was addressed to me. That deed, I think, is dated November. I do not know but think it is November. The deed is for one third, I think, of the stock in Venango County. It is only acknowledged, and everything seems legal about it. It was recorded. I do not known when. I paid no attention to it at all when I saw the thing but threw it in a drawer. I do not know that there was any deed of trust for my sister. That is all I know about it. I have not seen [?] it since. I left it in a drawer & never gave it another thought.

Do not know what company he was interested in, but Mr. Joe Simons knows all about it. He was for some time his agent. They dissolved connections and Simons went on his own responsibility. When they shut the well up, I think that ended their connection.

Q. Who else was connected in the oil business with him?

A. I do not know. The other two were John Ellsler and Reuben Meers. I think that is his name. They would not agree and works were stopped for some time. Ellsler lives in Cleveland, Ohio, [and] is a manager of a theatre. That is all the connection which he had with John. They held stock together & had a difficulty. Meers I think lives on the premises.

Q. Did your brother say anything about leaving part of it in trust for your sister?

A. No, sir. I have a sister Rosalie. He told me some time ago that he had given her some shares in oil stock, and that it had turned out much more valuable than he had any idea of.

Q. Did he ever give you any idea of what portion of the stock he gave you?

A. No, sir. I had an idea that he gave me more than a few shares. I think it was in February last that he told me about giving our sister the stock.

Q. When did he tell you that it had turned out more valuable than he had supposed it would?

A. At that time. I do not know whether she was aware that she possessed it at the time. She lives at my brother Edwin's house.

3. *Junius B. Booth, Jr., Diary for 1865*[11]

APRIL

15. [Cincinnati, Ohio] played Every night up to this date. This morn news came of the death of the President & John's deed last night in Washington. The excitement was so great that I remained in the Hotel till the night of Monday the 17th.

17. 10 PM. left for home, left my things with Nil Kaison*.

19. Arrived at Pha. at 12 M. Great excitement. Informed the US Marshall [*sic*] of my presence & Maj Ruggles,[†] who searched the house for John

23. Read a false ac[count] of the letter I wrote to John from Ciniti on the 12th.

25. Arrested on the newspaper report & taken to Washington.

26. In close confinement Room 14, Old Carrol [Prison], Col. Wood, Supt.

27. J. S. Clarke brought in. Kept like malefactor in a small room & on prison fare, forbid to speak to anyone or see a paper. Since learned that John was shot in Va. on the above date. Kept [in] close [confinement] till May 8th. lst from Ap. 26 to May 5th in close, then J. S. Clarke was put in with me & we allowed to go into the yard [for exercise].

MAY

6. Wrote a statement of all I knew regarding John to Sec. [of War] E. Stanton. Sent out & got my meals from Mrs. Whitney[‡] till the 10 of June.

---

*Cornelius Cassin, an acquaintance who lived in Cincinnati.

†Samuel G. Ruggles, chief of police.

‡George H. Whitney and family ran a restaurant on "A" Street on Capitol Hill.

27. John [S. Clarke] released. I detained till further investigation to see if anything might transpire to implicate me. Judge Holt said he had not seen my letter of the 12 [of April] or my statement to Stanton. Promised to do so & release me immediately.

31. Passed my time reading Spencer's works and such books as I could lay hands on. Many of the Prisoners have left & those remaining have more liberty. Much rain & quite cool weather. Bugs and roaches in abundance. Edwin came on to the trial & dined with me in 14. Stuart saw Holt for me.

J U N E

10. June, from the 1st to the 10th, the same. Daily hopes of release.

10. Joined the mess of Room 25—Delaney, Dr. S. S. Wheeler, Dr. Strigen & Arthur Cann.* Very hot, intolerably hot.

22. Informed of my release. Hemper of Pha presented a petition & letters to the Sec. of War from David Paul Brown,† J. H. Brewster, & other leading Philadelphians, which doubtless expedited it, together with Stuart's letters to Ast. Sec. [of War] Danna [sic].

22. After eight long weeks of imprisonment, left for Pha. at 7 pm.

23. 3 A.M., ar[rived] in Pha & found all up waiting for me. Ed[win] an[d] family.

24 to 28. Busy keeping cool & Enjoying my freedom and writing a statement for the Press, but found it might be too true to please the arbitrary Despotism of military rule. Resolved not to publish till the laws again protect the Citizen & the Bastille

---

*Dr. G. M. Delaney and Dr. Emil Stieger were civilian prisoners. Stieger, of Monroe, Wisconsin, was charged with defaming the government. Dr. Seth S. Wheeler was an army surgeon.

†David Paul Brown (1795–1872) was a leading criminal lawyer and author of *Sertorius*, a play whose title role the elder Booth had often performed.

thrown open. I hope to God never again to be [thus] used in a land having any pretensions to liberty. The history of the U. S. B. [United States Bastille, i.e., Old Capitol Prison] would rival its prototype of France & not displace it in injustice. But the truth would not be believed & a man would be called a traitor who would tell the truth, so bigotted [*sic*] are the mob. . . .

Asia Booth Clarke

Asia's description of the events of 1865 is given in her memoir of her brother. However, the following three documents, one given to the public and two to her friend Jean, are worthy of reprinting.

1. Extract from the introduction to *Booth Memorials. Passages, Incidents, and Anecdotes in the Life of Junius Brutus Booth, (the Elder.) By His Daughter* (1866).[12]

[Philadelphia]
[Summer, 1865]

A calamity, without precedent, has fallen upon our country! We, of all famliies, secure in domestic love and retirement, are stricken desolate! The name we would have enwreathed with laurels is dishonored by a *son*—'his well-beloved—his bright boy Absalom!'

2. *Asia B. Clarke to Jean Anderson*[13]

Philadelphia
May 22, 1865

My Dear Jean,

I have received both of your letters, and although feeling the kindness of your sympathy, could not compose my thoughts to write. I can give you no idea of the desolation which has fallen upon us. The sorrow of his [John's] death is very bitter, but the disgrace is far heavier—Already people are asserting that it is a political affair—the work of the bloody rebellion—the enthusiastic love of country, etc., but I am afraid to us it will always be a crime.

Junius and John Clarke have been two weeks to-day confined in the old Capital-prison Washington for no complicity or evidence—Junius wrote an innocent letter from Cincinnati, which by a wicked misconstruction has been the cause of his arrest. He begged [John Wilkes Booth] to quit the oil business and attend to his profession, not knowing the 'oil' signified conspiracy in Washington as it has since been proved that all employed in the plot, passed themselves off as 'oil merchants.'

John Clarke was arrested for having in his house a package of papers upon which he had never laid his hands or his eyes, but after the occurrence when I produced them, thinking it was a will put here for safe keeping—John took them to the U. S. marshall [*sic*], who reported to headquarters, hence this long imprisonment for two entirely innocent men.

I would not object at present to have back for my private use all the money they have squandered on Sanitary Commissions, Hospital Endowments, Relief of Soldiers Widows, and the like, for the good done by them as actors and citizens goes for nothing towards proving their innocence, and it might well have been tendered to a better purpose.

I suppose they will be examined at the leisure of the Court and return home to be nursed through a spell of illness—as one Gent has done who was released last week, and whose arrest proved only a farce as General somebody in authority expressed it. Poor old country, she has seen her best days, and I care not how soon I turn my back upon her shores forever. It is the history of the [Roman] Republic over again.

I was shocked and grieved to see the names of Michael O'Laughlin and Samuel Arnold. I am still some surprised to learn that all engaged in the plot are Roman Catholics.* John

---

*Mary Surratt and her son John, together with Dr. Samuel A. Mudd, were Catholics. O'Laughlen and Samuel Arnold were Methodist, Lewis Powell a Baptist, and George Atzerodt a Lutheran.

Wilkes was of that faith—preferably—and I was glad that he had fixed his faith on one religion for he was always of a pious mind and I won't speak of his qualities, you knew him.

My health is very delicate at present, but I seem completely numbed and hardened in sorrow.

The report of Blanche and Edwin [breaking their engagement] are without truth, their marriage not to have been until September, and I do not think it will be postponed so that it is a long way off yet. Edwin is here with me. Mother went home to N. Y. last week. She has been with me until he came.

I told you I believe that Wilkes was engaged to Miss Hale. They were most devoted lovers and she has written heartbroken letters to Edwin about it. Their marriage was to have been in a year, when she promised to return from Spain for him, either with her father or without him, that was the decision only a few days before the fearful calamity. Some terrible oath hurried him to this wretched end. God help him. Remember me to all and write often.

Yours every time,
Asia

3. *Asia B. Clarke to Jean Anderson*[14]

Philadelphia
February 15, 1866

My Dear Jean,

I received your unusually long letter and need not tell you how glad I was to find you had not forgotten me although I have been silent so long. I have had little heart to write or talk, or hold intercourse with any human being, but as time wears off the keenest edge of grief, so I have recovered somewhat.

I feel as if I had been stunned by some blow that I could not perceive or understand. Let it go with the past year. It don't [sic] bear dwelling on. . . .

I hope you won't change your mind about coming. I was not able to extend you much courtesy [when you visited] before, and I fear you felt it. However, you are sensible enough to allot any seeming coldness to my all absorbing troubles, not to any defect in my love for you.

Bless you all.

Ever your friend,
Asia

John S. Clarke

Clarke wrote the following statements, both of considerable interest, in the spring of 1865. In the first he asks fellow actor Lewis Baker to represent him at an indignation meeting of the theatrical profession in Philadelphia. The second document is the statement he gave in prison to federal investigators.

1. John S. Clarke to Lewis Baker[15]

[Philadelphia]
[April 21, 1865]

To Lewis Baker,

I beg that you will do me the especial favor to represent me at the meeting of our profession today.

The affliction under which I am suffering, worse than death, prevents my personal attendance. Proclaim my entire concurrence with any measure expressive of sympathy for the loss of our lamented President, loyalty to our government, or any other steps the wisdom of the meeting may think proper to take.

Yours,
J. S. Clarke

2. "Affidavit of John S. Clarke"[16]

[Washington]
May 6, 1865

I have not seen John Wilkes Booth since February 1865. I have no recollection of receiving but one letter from him in four years, which was *purely upon a theatrical matter.* I have had no conversation with him upon political subjects for at least two years, as our views were entirely different.

I am and have always been entirely loyal to the United States Government—and have had no sympathy with man or woman of rebellious principles. Contrary to a fixed rule of my own, I have repeatedly volunteered (gratuitously) my professional services in aid of the United States Sanitary Commission, and made many private contributions beneficial to the Federal cause.

I do and have always believed every member of the Booth family (save Wilkes) to be in sentiment and feeling loyal to the U. S. Government.

John Wilkes Booth has repeatedly within, say, two years left at my house in care of his sister (my wife) large envelopes sealed and directed to himself, saying for 'safe keeping' as he was obliged to travel through the far west to meet his professional engagements, invariably stating that they contained 'stocks etc.' These envelopes have remained sometimes months, and he has called for them.

About the latter part of November '64, while I was acting in New York, he left a sealed envelope at my house in Philadelphia in this way. During January he again visited my house and asked for it, took it and shortly after returned it (or a similar one), and it was again placed as usual in my safe.

On the Saturday Afternoon following the assassination of the President, Mrs. Booth, the mother, came to my house from New York. The whole family was of course much depressed and excited. On Sunday Afternoon we thought of the envelope, and Mrs. Booth, my wife and I determined to open it.

We found the letter which was published—and for his Mother a letter, 5–20 bonds to amount of $3000., Phila. City 6s to amount of $1000—and an assignment of some oil land in Penna. to his brother Junius, and nothing more. I kept these papers in my possession during Monday, thinking that probably the authorities would enquire at the residences of his family for his papers—no one called—On Tuesday I handed them over to the United States Marshal, suggesting to him that if consistent [with the public good] I should like to cause to be published the letter for his mother as in that he exonerated his entire family from any sympathy with his secession propensities. I was surprised the next day to find the other letter published and not the one for his mother which I suggested should be made public.

Upon the arrival at my house of Junius B. Booth on Wednesday 19th April, from Cincinnati, I casually remarked, at such a time a *Booth* entering my house might cause a talk, whereupon Junius instantly desired that his arrival should be made known. I called at Marshal Milward's [*sic*]—he was out. On hearing that I had called the Marshal visited me the next morning, and I introduced to him Mr. Junius B. Booth on Thursday April 20th.

Sworn to and subscribed before me this 6th day of May 1865.

L. C. Turner,

J[udge] Advocate

[P.S.] Born in Baltimore, Sep. 3rd 1832

Philadelphia has been my residence since August 1852.

J. S. Clarke

JOSEPH ADRIAN BOOTH

"Joe" Booth was the youngest of the Booth children. He suffered several episodes of depression when young. During a crisis in 1862 John feared he might attempt suicide. Instead, Joe went on a round-the-world trip, visiting Europe, Australia, and California. The apparent coincidence of his departing San Francisco for New York on April 13, 1865, the day before Lincoln's assassination, led to his arrest upon arrival in the east. He was released shortly after giving the following statement. He became a physician later in life.

1. "*Examination of Joseph Adrian Booth Before Maj. Gen. [John A.] Dix. . . .*"[17]

New York City
May 12, 1865

J. A. Booth [says] I have never been brought up to any particular business. I have read medicine for a time. I was in Wells, Fargo's employ in San Francisco.

Q. For what period were you in their employ?
A. A little over a year.

Q. Beginning when and ending when?
A. I think it was June, one year ago—not quite a year.

Q. June of '63 or '64?
A. June of '63 [misstatement, corrected below].

Q. That would be two years last June?
A. Yes, sir.

Q. When did you leave them?
A. I left on the 9th or 10th of last month.

Q. You were with them from June '63 to April '65.
A. Yes, sir. It has been only a year—June '64. I came from Australia.

Q. What capacity were you in with them?
A. I was letter clerk—carrying letters.

Q. Why did you leave them?
A. I disliked the business very much. The city is very hilly, and I had a great part of the city to go over. I was on foot. Had to carry a great many letters around.

Q. You were a letter deliverer in the city of San Francisco?
A. Yes, sir. That was my business.

Q. What day did you leave San Francisco?
A. The 13th of April.

Q. You came directly here?

A. Intending to come directly here.

Q. Where did you hear of the President's assassination?

A. At Panama. Got full particulars when I [crossed the isthmus and] got [to] the other side in Aspinwall.

Q. Have you had any intercourse with your brother?

A. I had one letter while in Australia and one while in California. That one is Australia was three years ago. In California was five months ago.

Q. He was here at that time—the last was written from here?

A. I do not know whether it was dated in New York. I think it was in Pennsylvania somewhere.

Q. Have you only heard from him twice in four years?

A. Yes, sir.

Q. Have you been in California all the time?

A. I was in Australia a portion of the time.

Q. Did you get both letters from this section of the country?

A. Yes sir—United States.

Q. Did you preserve the letters?

A. No, sir, I didn't. The letters were of no importance at all—just congratulating me on my return to California and my success in business.

Q. What did you do in Australia?

A. I went out there with this quite boyish freak to make my fortune. I tried mining for a time. Was on a sheep and cattle station, northern part—clerk in the station.

Q. What is your age, Mr. Booth?

A. I am 23, sir [actual age, 25].

Q. Your brother John was older?

A. Yes, sir.

Q. You are the youngest of your family?

A. Yes, sir.

Q. You run [*sic*] away from John in this city?

A. Yes, sir. That was about four and a half years ago. That was the time I went to Australia.

Q. Had he any guardianship over you?

A. No, sir—none at all. I was with him transacting business with him at the Theatre. I was troubled in mind and worried. I always had a sort of desire to travel—had money and left at the time to England to see my brother Edwin there, and with the intention of seeing my grandmother just before she died. She lived in Reading. She was dead a couple of weeks before I got there.

Q. Have you any political associations in California, Mr. Booth?

A. No, sir.

Q. Of any kind?

A. No, sir. I never was anything of a politician. I never studied politics much.

Q. Have you taken any part since this Rebellion broke out in public affairs?

A. No, sir. I have always felt loyal in regard to wishing the restoration of the country to its former . . . [answer not completed].

Q. You have had no association in California with persons hostile to the government?

A. There is one or two persons who came from the same part of the country I was from; I used to know them—just merely used to talk to each other. There was never any political conversation to my knowledge.

Q. Have you ever heard anything in California from anyone in regard to attempts to murder the President or members of the Cabinet, or commit any acts of violence of any kind to overthrow the government?

A. No, sir. I have never heard of anything such as that. I never was so astonished in anything as when I got to Panama to hear what had occurred—and my own brother.

. . .

Q. Did you ever quarrel with John at that time you went away?

A. Yes, sir. We had a little unpleasant feeling.

Q. What was the cause of that quarrel?

A. He thought I was not attending to his business.

Q. You was [*sic*] acting as agent for him at that time?

A. Yes, sir.

Q. He was playing an engagement?

A. Yes, sir. At Wallack's old Theatre (now the Broadway).

Q. Did you perform yourself?

A. No, sir.

Q. You never was [*sic*] on the stage?

A. Yes, sir—once or twice, but never to make it a business. Once in Philadelphia and once in Buffalo some years ago. I was travelling with my brother Edwin. I just done [*sic*] it because the actors were not sufficient in number to play the piece. Done it out of courtesy.

Q. How long did you travel as agent for John Wilkes Booth?

A. That was the only time I was with him—it was during my stay in the city. That was between three and four years ago.

Q. How long was it after you left him that you heard from him?

A. It was about two or three months.

Q. Did you write him from England?

A. Yes, sir.

. . . .

Q. In that last letter that John wrote you did he offer you any inducements to come home—the one you received in California?

A. He wished me to stick to my business—to not roam any more round the world. He offered me no inducements to come home.

Q. Said nothing about your returning to the States—New York—or home did he?

A. I do not remember anything.

Q. Was your brother Junius in California when you arrived there?

A. Yes, sir.

Q. How long has Junius been on here?

A. About a year, I think.

Q. Did he get this situation for you at Wells Fargo & Co's?

A. Yes, sir.

Q. Did you ever hear him spoken of there as a loyal man or not?

A. Everyone gave that opinion—he was very loyal.

Q. You always heard him spoken of as a loyal man?

A. Yes, sir.

Q. Is his family on here?

A. He has one daughter—a child?

Q. What is the name of that child

A. Mary Booth—no middle name—Yes, her name is Mary Rosalie—she was named after my sister Rosalie.

Q. You know that Junius has given up all his business in California intending to make this his home—or there?

A. I do not know what length of time he contemplated staying here. His family is here—came on with him.

Q. Is that all your baggage?

A. Yes, sir.

Q. You said you left the employment of Wells Fargo about the 1st of April?
A. It was the first week of April.

Q. And got away the 13th.
A. Yes, sir.

Q. You left them for the purpose of coming here?
A. Yes, sir—intended to try to get into the office in this city.

Q. You resigned there?
A. Yes, sir.

Q. Was not dismissed from their service?
A. Not at all.

Q. What amount of money—did you not have some money belonging to Wilkes in your possession when you went away?
A. Not much—a few dollars. Had money of my own.

Q. What is the amount you had when you started away from here?
A. About $115 altogether.

Q. What portion of that belonged to Wilkes?
A. About $3 or $4. I was entitled to more than that as my salary.
. . . .

Q. Have you ever been insane, Mr. Booth?
A. Yes, sir.

Q. For how long a time?
A. For several months. I was [also] insane in Panama.

Q. On your return?
A. Yes, sir. That news made me insane.

Q. You was [sic] troubled before you went away from time to time?

A. Yes, sir.

Q. Have you any idea how long you was [*sic*] troubled on your way here?

A. Two or three days aboard ship, when I heard the news. Two or three days out before I began to get my thinking faculties.

Q. You have had several attacks of it in your lifetime?
A. Yes, sir.

Q. Do you remember how old you was [*sic*] when you had the first attack?

A. No, sir. About 10 or 12 I think.

Q. Have you ever been confined for that?
A. No, sir. It was melancholy insanity.

[*Added into the original manuscript*: Sergt. Young remarked that when Joseph ran away, Wilkes left his likeness and was under the impression that he might commit suicide.]

Q. Have you no papers of your own?
A. No, sir.

Q. Had you not any papers about you when you was [*sic*] arrested on board ship?

A. No, sir.

Q. Any in your pocketbook?

A. I have no papers to my knowledge in it. (Examines it.) No, sir. (It was stated that he had been searched and no papers found on his person besides his passport.) I received $75 a month at Wells Fargo—boarded myself—boarded right across the street from the office—had a room to myself. The party's name who kept the house was—cannot think of his name now. . . .

Q. Did you not get any recommendation from Wells Fargo when you left?

A. No, sir.

Q. Did you ask for one?

A. I wrote to June, if he would not get me into the office here in the city.

Q. Didn't you ask for any sort of recommendation when you left?

A. No, sir.

Q. Was it known on board the steamer that you was [*sic*] the brother of Wilkes?

A. Yes, sir. Several asked me how had he looked, etc.

Q. Was your insanity spoken of by anyone?

A. No, sir—I do not think it was.

Q. You have no friend with you who came on on board the steamer?

A. No, sir.

. . . .

Q. I want him to state where he was when he heard the news of the assassination and all about it.

A. I came in the *Moses Taylor*. I got ashore at Panama. I think the day we got in bulletins were stuck upon the corners, little slips telegraphed from the other side—[the] regular steamer that came from New York brought the news. I saw the statement. It said a man named Booth. I did not think anything of that. I knew there was [*sic*] a hundred Booths. In the afternoon an additional telegraph came and gave full particulars. Then was the first moment I could imagine it was a brother of mine done it.

Q. Did it say John Wilkes Booth?

A. Yes, sir. The first said "a man named Booth." As soon as we got to Aspinwall I saw the papers, full particulars.

Q. Did you have any conversation with anyone in Aspinwall before you heard it was John Wilkes Booth?

A. [No one] except the passengers. They asked me if I knew it was a brother of mine. I said yes. I did not deny it.

Q. What passengers—those going over to Aspinwall with you?

A. Yes, sir.

Q. Did you see anyone from the other side who had come from New York?

A. No, sir. They had got there at five o'clock in the afternoon—we left the next morning.

Q. You did not converse with any of those passengers?

A. With regard to it?

Q. Yes, sir.

A. No, sir. Only with those who were coming this way with me. As soon as they got out of the train, they went right aboard the ship.

Q. How was the assassination spoken of by those on board?

A. As a most horrible, bloody thing.

Q. None in favor?

A. None in favor of it.

Q. None that seemed pleased with it?

A. No, sir. I did not notice one.

NOTES

1. Records of the Attorney General's Office, General Records, Letters Received Files (1809–1870), General Records of the Department of Justice, RG 60, National Archives, Archives II, College Park, Md.

2. This document is found with Booth's letter to his mother in the Justice Department records.

3. *New York Clipper,* April 22, 1865; William Winter, *Life and Art of Edwin Booth* (New York: MacMillan, 1893), p. 272.

4. Reprinted in "Edwin Booth and Lincoln," *Century Magazine,* New Series, vol. 55 (April 1909): pp. 919–920; portions in brackets supplied from Washington *Evening Star,* April 2, 1914.

5. Edwin Booth Misc. Mss., The New-York Historical Society, New York City, and reproduced through the courtesy of the society. John B. Murray owned a prominent brokerage firm and lived with his wife in a mansion on Fifth Avenue.

6. Edwina Booth Grossmann, *Edwin Booth: Recollections by His Daughter and Letters to Her and to His Friends* (New York: Century Co., 1894), pp. 172–173.

7. Grossmann, pp. 227–228. Capen (1804–1886) was an author and former postmaster in Boston who was writing "History of Democracy."

8. Reproduced by courtesy of the Hampden-Booth Library, The Players, New York City.

9. Investigation and Trial Papers, M-599, reel 2, frames 0260–0268. A summary of this document with a few additional points is found on reel 4, frames 0117–0120. Further remarks on his April 12 letter to John are found at reel 2, frames 0257–0259.

10. Investigation and Trial Papers, M-599, reel 3, frames 0741–0745.

11. Special Collections, Mugar Memorial Library, Boston University.

12. Introduction, p. vii.

13. Peale Museum collection.

14. Peale Museum collection.

15. *Washington Chronicle,* April 23, 1865.

16. Investigation and Trial Papers, M-599, reel 7, frames 0408–0412.

17. Union Provost Marshal's File of One-Name Papers Relating to Citizens, RG 109, available handily as M-345, National Archives. The

interrogation is printed in John C. Brennan, "John Wilkes Booth's Enigmatic Brother Joseph," *Maryland Historical Magazine,* vol. 78 (Spring 1983): pp. 26–29, with some editing of repetitious material.

BIBLIOGRAPHICAL NOTE

A well-written introduction to the Booth family is found in Gene Smith, *American Gothic: The Story of America's Legendary Theatrical Family - Junius, Edwin, and John Wilkes Booth* (New York: Simon & Schuster, 1992). Stanley Kimmel's *The Mad Booths of Maryland* (Indianapolis: Bobbs Merrill, 1940: revised edition, 1969) is a work along the same lines, older but still useful. For Booth's parents and childhood environment one should turn to Stephen H. Archer's skillfully researched *Junius Brutus Booth: American Prometheus* (Carbondale, Ill.: Southern Illinois University Press, 1992).

A highly-readable life of Edwin Booth is Eleanor Ruggles' *Prince of Players* (New York: W. W. Norton, 1953). This life was made into a 1955 motion picture staring Richard Burton as Edwin. An important new biography is being prepared by Daniel Watermeier. There are no extended biographical studies of J. B. Booth, Jr., Joseph Booth, Asia Booth Clarke, or John S. Clarke.

The most recent life of Lincoln's assassin is by Francis Wilson, *John Wilkes Booth* (Boston: Houghton Mifflin, 1929). Very dated, it is nevertheless worthwhile reading. Another older title dealing largely with Booth is George S. Bryan, *The Great American Myth* (New York: Carrick & Evans, 1940), a book of solid research and judgment. Booth's acting career is traced by Gordon Samples in *Lust for Fame: The Stage Career of John Wilkes Booth* (Jefferson, N.C.: McFarland, 1982). Timothy S. Good, *We Saw Lincoln Shot: One Hundred Eyewitness Accounts* (Jackson: University Press of Mississippi, 1995), contains recollections of Booth on April 14, 1865.

There has been a great deal of shoddy historical writing on the Lincoln assassination over the years. William Hanchett, *The Lincoln Murder Conspiracies* (Urbana & Chicago: University of Illinois Press, 1983), is a good guide through this thicket. Thomas Reed Turner, *Beware the People Weeping: Public Opinion and the Assassination of Abraham Lincoln* (Baton Rouge: Louisiana State University Press, 1982), asks and answers numerous important questions about the assassination. The intelligence and evenhandedness of these two authors are notable. William A. Tidwell, with James O. Hall and David W. Gaddy, in *Come Retribution: The Confederate Secret Service and the Assassination of Lincoln* (Jackson: University Press of Mississippi, 1988), seek to establish Booth within the framework of Southern plots against Lincoln. Tidwell's recent book *April '65: Confederate Covert Action in the American Civil War* (Kent, Ohio, and London: Kent State University Press, 1995), continues to develop the background of this approach.

INDEX